THE WORLD of
ORTHODOX JUDAISM

THE WORLD of ORTHODOX JUDAISM

ELI W. SCHLOSSBERG

A JASON ARONSON BOOK

ROWMAN & LITTLEFIELD PUBLISHERS, INC.
Lanham • Boulder • New York • Toronto • Oxford

A JASON ARONSON BOOK

ROWMAN & LITTLEFIELD PUBLISHERS, INC.

Published in the United States of America
by Rowman & Littlefield Publishers, Inc.
A wholly owned subsidiary of The Rowman & Littlefield Publishing Group, Inc.
4501 Forbes Boulevard, Suite 200, Lanham, Maryland 20706
www.rowmanlittlefield.com

PO Box 317
Oxford
OX2 9RU, UK

Copyright © 1996 by Eli W. Schlossberg
First Rowman & Littlefield edition 2004

All rights reserved. No part of this publication may be reproduced, stored in a retrieval system, or transmitted in any form or by any means, electronic, mechanical, photocopying, recording, or otherwise, without the prior permission of the publisher.

British Library Cataloguing in Publication Information Available

Library of Congress Cataloging-in-Publication Data

Schlossberg, Eli W.
 The world of Orthodox Judaism / Eli W. Schlossberg.
 p. cm.
 Includes index.
 ISBN 0-7657-5955-1 (alk. paper)
 1. Orthodox Judaism. 2. Jews—Dietary laws. I. Title.
BM570.S35 1997
296.8'32—dc20   96-41189

Printed in the United States of America

♾™ The paper used in this publication meets the minimum requirements of American National Standard for Information Sciences—Permanence of Paper for Printed Library Materials, ANSI/NISO Z39.48-1992.

*To
my father*

Acknowledgments

This book is written in honor of my dad, Fred A. Schlossberg. One of the world's finest fathers, Dad was the first to teach me about our beautiful religious heritage, and today he continues to inspire me by example. A deeply religious Orthodox Jew, he serves as a role model for me and for every Orthodox Jewish businessman.

Although he is a consummate entrepreneur and executive, Dad modestly regards himself simply as a salesman. It is he who schooled me in my field of expertise, the specialty gourmet food business. Dad arrived in America in 1938, and since entering the food industry in 1942, he has been buying and selling imported gourmet specialties. To me, he is the world's best salesman. Over the past 54 years, together with my wonderful mom and enterprising grandmother, he built the family business. He continues selling fine foods today, calling regularly on accounts he has been servicing for decades.

Each day I thank God for giving me such marvelous parents, who provided me with a wonderful upbringing. I attribute any success that I may encounter in life to the exceptional educational opportunities my parents provided for me and to the love they continue to bestow on me and my family each and every day.

Contents

To the Reader	xiii
Portrait of an Orthodox Jew	xv
What Is an Orthodox Jew?	1
Man to God . . . Man to Man	2
Institutions of Orthodox Jewish Life	5
Prayer	5
The Synagogue	6
Torah Study and Education	6
Mitzvos and *Minhagim*: Laws and Customs	7
Tzedakah and *Chesed*: Charity and Good Deeds	9
Israel	11
Orthodox Types and Lifestyles	13
Chassidic Jews	13
The Non-Chassidic Jews	15

Shabbos—The Sabbath	17
What is *Shabbos*?	17
Sabbath Observance	18
A Typical *Shabbos*	20
Dealing with Sabbath Prohibitions	22
The *Eruv*	23
Business	25
Emergency Situations	26
Holidays	29
Sketches of the Jewish Holidays	29
Rosh Hashana	29
Yom Kippur	30
Sukkos	30
Passover	32
Shavuos	33
Purim	34
Chanukah	34
Tisha B'Av	35
Restrictions on Work during Holidays	35
Orthodox Jewish Celebrations	37
General Remarks on Dress and Behavior	37
Bris (Circumcision)	38
Bar Mitzvah and Bat Mitzvah	38
Courtship and the Marriage Process	39
The *Shidduch*	40
Weddings	43
Funerals	45
Everything You Ever Wanted to Know About Keeping Kosher, But Were Afraid to Ask	47
Portrait of a Kosher Gourmet	47
Food in Judaism	48

Who Else Eats Kosher . . . And What is Kosher?	51
Does Kosher Mean the Same as Healthy?	54
Why Do Jews Keep Kosher?	55
What Makes Food Kosher?	**57**
Some Basic Rules of Kashruth	60
Kosher Species	60
Milk and Eggs	61
Cheese	61
Kosher Meat: The Long Road from Farm to Freezer	61
Shechitah	61
Glatt Kosher	62
Veins and Forbidden Fats	63
Hindquarters	63
Koshering meat	64
Meat, Dairy and *Pareve*	64
Other Products	66
Wine and Grape Juice	66
Soft Drinks and Alcoholic Beverages	66
Fresh Fruits and Vegetables	67
Canned Fruits and Vegetables	67
Breads and Other Baked Goods	68
Oils, Fats, and Margarine	69
Condiments, Sauces, etc.	69
Kosher for Passover	69
The Kosher Kitchen	70
Kosher Eating	**73**
Kosher Bloopers	74
Inviting an Orthodox Guest to Your Home or Restaurant	76
Eating Out of Your Suitcase, or the Joys of Kosher Travel	**81**

Summing Up 89

Glossary of Hebrew and Yiddish Terms 91

Index 101

To the Reader

If you work with an Orthodox Jew or live near an Orthodox Jewish neighborhood, you have probably noticed that observant Jews seem to act in some unusual ways. If you have not had the opportunity to ask your Orthodox employees, coworkers, friends, or neighbors why it is they do those seemingly strange things—or you have been too polite to ask—this booklet is for you. I hope it will answer some of your questions about Orthodox Jews, their traditions, and the lifestyle they follow.

Portrait of an Orthodox Jew

One of your coworkers—let's call him Bernie—wears a skullcap. You sometimes see him sitting in the company cafeteria moving his lips after finishing his lunch. Occasionally, you see him facing the wall in his office, eyes closed, swaying back and forth. When the whole office goes to a fancy restaurant for lunch, he may eat in the office, or if he comes along, he only orders a soda, an iced tea, or perhaps a fresh fruit cup or a plain salad with no dressing. Strangely, his rotund shape suggests that he can't really be on a diet. On Friday mornings in the winter, he shows up at the office early and leaves an hour-and-a-half before anybody else, but in the summer months, when most people leave early on Friday, he stays late. You might think that Bernie is a little strange, but he seems quite normal when you talk to him.

This strange behavior is because Bernie, like me, is an Orthodox Jew. He doesn't wear his skullcap to keep his head warm—it's a *yarmulke*,[1] and it reminds him that there is always Someone above, whose laws must be obeyed by him at all times. When he appears to be talking to himself after lunch, he's not complaining about the boss—he's actually thanking God.[2] When he stands and sways in his office, he's not practicing calisthenics—he's praying. He's not eating the same lunch as everyone else in the company because it's not kosher. He leaves early on Fridays in the winter because the Sabbath begins early then, and he must get home in time to observe that holy day. However, during the long summer days, when the Sabbath starts later, he is able to stay and work late.

Your conversations with Bernie show that he is very worldly. He is up-to-date on current events and sports. His work is thoroughly professional, and he is a well-educated and cultured person. He is different in that in his daily life he demonstrates that his ultimate values are belief in God and subservience to the laws of the Torah[3], which is the supreme guiding force in all of his actions.

One day a week, from sunset on Friday to Saturday night, he withdraws from the world of work. He enters totally into a different world that is equally real to him: the spiritual world of the holy Sabbath, with its own set of strict laws and customs. He devotes a major part of his time

---

[1] When you find an unfamiliar term, consult the glossary beginning on p. 91.

[2] Orthodox Jews often do not write out the Divine name in full in order not to transgress the commandment "Thou shalt not take the Lord's name in vain." The spellings in this book are the publisher's choice.

[3] The 613 commandments written in the Five Books of Moses, as explained and elaborated by the traditional Oral Law.

and resources to passing his values and beliefs on to his children. He educates them in the same tradition he follows, training them in the importance of respect for elders and for their fellow man. By passing on this way of life, he hopes to forge one more link in a chain of tradition that goes back thousands of years.

In the following chapters, I have tried to answer many of the most-common questions people have about Orthodox Judaism and its practices. I begin with an account of the way the Sabbath, holidays, and family milestones are observed, then continue with a summary of the kosher dietary laws, and conclude with a discussion of some differing approaches within the world of Orthodox Judaism. I have attempted to explain in simple terms the principles behind many of its practices, the beliefs they illustrate, and how they affect the everyday life of Orthodox Jews.

What Is an Orthodox Jew?

Every child born to a Jewish mother is automatically Jewish, regardless of his or her father's religious status. A non-Jew may convert to Judaism by persuading an Orthodox rabbi of his or her sincere intent to accept the laws of Judaism and by following the conversion procedure detailed in the *Code of Jewish Law*. Converts who have followed this route, which involves a thorough Jewish education and many months of intensive training, are universally accepted as Jewish.

All Jews are expected to follow the laws of the Torah, the 613 commandments written in The Five Books of Moses, as explained and elaborated in detail by the traditional Oral Law taught by the rabbis of the Talmud and later. As in any religion, there are some individuals who are more observant and some who are less observant. In general terms, the degree of attachment to Torah traditions is indicated by the category of affiliation to religious groupings known as *Orthodox, Conservative,* and *Reform,* and, in addition, many Jews describe themselves as nonreligious, or secular. Within each category there is a wide range in the degree of religious observance by particular individuals. Comparing the three main religious groupings, Orthodox Jews are the most strict in their acceptance and observance of the 613 commandments mentioned in the Torah. Although many of these laws (for example, those dealing with the sacrificial services and many laws dealing with ritual purity) cannot be practiced today, Orthodox Jews still accept their validity and believe that one day, when the Messiah comes, it will be possible to resume them. The Conservative movement observes fewer of these laws, and the Reform movement observes fewer still. Again, it must be emphasized that every person with a mother who is truly Jewish is 100% Jewish, regardless of the personal level of religious observance.

Orthodox Jews are expected to observe the commandments of the Torah to their maximum ability. Strict observance of the Sabbath and the kosher laws are two of the most important and visible indications that people use to determine another Jew's religiosity, so that, in general, a Jew who keeps kosher and observes the Sabbath laws is called a *shomer Shabbos,* or *Sabbath observer,* and would be considered to be an Orthodox Jew.

MAN TO GOD ... MAN TO MAN

To be truly Orthodox requires complementing the life of service to God with a devotion to living in peace and harmony with other people. Orthodox Jews must be meticulous in their every action, striving for excellence in both the aspects of man to God and man to his fellow. They are expected always to serve as living examples of people who sanctify their Creator in all their actions. The way they conduct their lives in the roles of spouse, parent, child, friend, business person, employee, or professional should be strongly influenced by their religious beliefs. In all of their activities, work, recreation, or community service, God's existence must be weighed in every decision or action they take.

The great Orthodox rabbinical scholar of nineteenth-century Europe, Rabbi Samson Raphael Hirsch, wrote in his book *Horeb* about the overwhelming responsibility of the pious Jew to accept the yoke of religion. He explained that the yoke of religion is not overbearing, nor a bondage to a person. In fact, it frees a person from the greatest bondage of all—the bondage of man. Rabbi Hirsch's famous concept of Orthodox Judaism is called *Torah Im Derech Eretz*—Torah together with a livelihood. This credo means a combination of studying the Torah with living an economically productive and socially exemplary existence together with one's fellows. This is the way I have been taught that an Orthodox person must live. It is the way of life to which every Jew should aspire.

Institutions of Orthodox Jewish Life

PRAYER

Orthodox men are obligated to pray three times every day. It is preferable, but not absolutely necessary, to do so communally, as part of a group of at least ten men praying together—a minyan.

The morning service takes from a half hour to an hour, depending on the day of the week and the month. It may begin as early as the crack of dawn, and men who have to be at work early often go straight from the synagogue to their workplace.

The afternoon and evening services are much shorter, about ten to fifteen minutes with a minyan and perhaps less than ten minutes by oneself. The afternoon service should be completed before sunset. In synagogues, the evening service generally follows very shortly after the afternoon service, though it may be recited at any time until dawn the next day.

THE SYNAGOGUE

A synagogue that is used for congregational prayer need not be an imposing structure. An Orthodox synagogue can be any room large enough to hold ten men, the minimum number needed to recite prayers collectively. Men and women sit separately during prayers, and there must be a divider, or *mechitzah*, to separate the two sections. The synagogue must have an *Aron Kodesh*, a Holy Ark, which is the cabinet used to hold the Torah scroll (*Sefer Torah*) used during prayer services on the Sabbath and holidays and every Monday and Thursday morning. The Ark is on the eastern wall of the synagogue, and the entire congregation faces that way while standing to recite the most important prayers. The Torah is brought out to be read from the *bimah*, a platform or table that is placed in the center of Orthodox synagogues. Many synagogues have a permanent cantor who leads the services on Sabbath and Holidays, although services may be led by any male above the age of Bar Mitzvah who is able to recite the prayers. Weekday services are generally led by a lay member of the congregation, often a mourner who has a special obligation to recite the kaddish, which is part of every prayer service.

TORAH STUDY AND EDUCATION

One of the fundamental pillars of Jewish life is study of the Torah and its religious laws. Orthodox men may be found studying the Talmud individually or in groups at any time from the predawn morning hours before services until the wee hours of the morning after midnight. This study is carried out both to become aware of the massively complex details of all areas of Jewish law and for its own sake, simply as a vital religious obligation.

In Orthodox circles today, boys and girls alike enjoy a high standard of religious education. Jewish day schools are private schools that provide Jewish children with a dual English and Hebrew, secular and religious studies program. Loosely affiliated with an organization called Torah Umesorah, at least one of these schools can be found in every major center of Jewish population in the United States. These schools provide a combination of high-quality Jewish and secular education from kindergarten to twelfth grade. Some of them are very large institutions. For example, Bais Yaakov School for Girls in Baltimore has over 1200 students.

To cover their heavy dual load, it is not uncommon for Orthodox children to be in school from 9 am to 6 pm five days a week, plus half of a day on Sundays. After twelve years of this intensive education, many Orthodox boys and girls continue their Jewish education in yeshivos (rabbinical seminaries) for boys and teachers' seminaries for girls. This intensive religious education is often accompanied by secular college studies.

MITZVOS AND *MINHAGIM*: LAWS AND CUSTOMS

The Orthodox way of life is based on the Torah. This term encompasses the written Torah, or The Five Books of Moses, and the Oral Torah. The written Torah contains 613 mitzvos, or Divine commandments. Some mitzvos are positive, requiring Jews to do certain things; others are prohibitions, forbidding them to do other things. It is impossible to understand how to carry out many of these commandments simply by reading the Bible. They are explained in great detail by the Oral Torah, which is the collection of explanations and amplifications explained by God to Moses and handed down through all the generations since his time through the prophets and then the rabbis. The most important document of the Oral Torah is the Talmud. All Orthodox religious law, as it develops to meet new situations, is based on the discussions found in the Talmud and the decisions codified by later rabbis in the *Shulchan Aruch*, the authoritative Code of Jewish Law.

Orthodox Jews observe the mitzvos because they are commanded by God. Some mitzvos are easier to understand than others, but all are equally binding. Let me describe two little-known *mitzvos* that are still practiced today.

Shatnez is a negative mitzvah. The word means a mixture of linen and wool, and the Torah forbids Jews to wear a garment containing such a mixture. This is a mitzvah that is impossible to explain rationally, but Orthodox Jews observe it faithfully. For example, when an Orthodox man buys a new suit, he takes it to a specially trained expert who scrutinizes the material and examines all the threads, buttonholes, and lining, perhaps even peering through a microscope, before he pronounces it free of *shatnez* and permissible to wear.

Shiluach Haken—sending away a mother bird—is a positive mitzvah. The Torah says that if someone finds a (kosher) bird's nest with eggs in it and wants the eggs, he must first send away the mother. The classic rabbinical commentators explain that although Jews are obligated to perform this *mitzvah* simply because it is a Divine commandment, it is possible to explain a reason for it. The reason is not that we feel sorry for the mother bird and don't want to upset her, because the best way not to upset her would be to leave the eggs alone. Rather, sending away the mother before taking the eggs will teach us that we must always act in a kind and merciful fashion, and if the Torah wants us to show this consideration even for birds, how much more must we be careful in our dealings with other people.

Minhag means a custom. Many of the things Orthodox Jews do are not actually commanded by the Torah, but are customs that have become generally accepted among Jews. Some *minhagim* have been so widely accepted that they have achieved the status of religious laws (for example, covering the head while praying). Other customs have become accepted among some Jewish communities, but not others. For example, Chassidic Jews generally dress in the same fashion as their forebears did in Eastern Europe, although most other Jews wear conventional Western dress. No Orthodox Jews eat dairy foods immediately after eating meat, but customs vary regarding the period they have to wait. Depending on the custom that prevailed in the place their family came from, they may wait anywhere from one hour to six hours. And on Passover, Ashkenazic Jews have accepted the custom to refrain from eating rice and beans, but Sephardic Jews have not accepted this restriction.

TZEDAKAH AND *CHESED*: CHARITY AND GOOD DEEDS

Jews are instructed by the Torah to be aware of the needs of the poor and downtrodden, particularly widows and orphans, and to provide both financial and emotional support. Two aspects of this fundamental *mitzvah* of Judaism are *tzedakah*—donating money for charitable purposes, and *gemilus chasodim*—donating personal time and effort to helping others.

Today Orthodox Jews tithe their net earnings or business profits based on the command of tithing that was obligatory during the biblical era, when the Temple was still standing. As well as helping needy individuals and families, priorities in Orthodox giving include financial support for building and operating Jewish religious educational institutions, synagogues, and *mikvaos* (ritual bath houses used by married women).

A host of voluntary organizations within the Orthodox community dedicate themselves not only to helping meet the financial needs of the poor but also to performing other acts of *chesed* (kindness and good deeds). For example, New York's Tomchei Shabbos and Baltimore's Ahavas Yisrael Charity Fund run kosher food banks that feed poor and needy families. Working together, men, women, and children donate thousands of hours of effort to helping the unfortunate. Many Orthodox businesspeople, doctors, lawyers, accountants, and other professionals volunteer their time and services to help their less fortunate fellows. Some volunteer activities of members of the Orthodox community include visiting the sick, aged, and homebound, assisting families with newborn babies by relieving the mother of cooking meals and other household chores, and helping needy families with interest-free loans.

The eagerness to engage in *tzedakah* and *chesed* is a feature of Jewish life that goes all the way back to the first Jew, the patriarch Abraham. This eagerness is a phenomenon without parallel in any other society of the twentieth century. All Jews, and the Orthodox in particular, can be proud of their voluntary contributions to their community and to the rest of humanity.

ISRAEL

The land of Israel occupies a special place in the heart of every Jew. It is the land that God promised to Abraham, Isaac, and Jacob. To Orthodox Jews, it has special significance as the only land where many of the *mitzvos* of the Torah can be carried out. Within the land of Israel, Jerusalem has a unique place as the site of the two Temples where the Kohanim (priests) and Levites performed the rites of Divine worship commanded in the Torah. For thousands of years, the daily prayers recited by Jews three times a day have expressed the wish for the coming of the Messiah and the rebuilding of the Holy Temple.

Today, Orthodox Jews are the majority of voluntary immigrants to Israel, and many post-high school Orthodox students spend time studying in yeshivos and women's seminaries before returning to live in America.

Orthodox Types and Life Styles

For the purpose of discussion here, an Orthodox Jew is one who follows all the commandments of the Torah to the best of his or her ability. According to Jewish tradition, the written Torah contains 613 commandments. No single individual can follow every one, because some are applicable only to men, some to women, some to members of priestly (Kohanim) or Levitical families, some only in the land of Israel, and some only when the Temple stands. What distinguishes the Orthodox Jew from his Conservative or Reform counterpart is the acceptance that all these laws are binding where they are applicable and that they should be strictly adhered to.

CHASSIDIC JEWS

If you have ever driven through the New York City communities of Williamsburg or Boro Park in Brooklyn, or

Monsey, Spring Valley, or New Square in Rockland County, you undoubtedly have seen many members of this fascinating group of devout Jews. They dress, regardless of season, in the long black coats and wide-brimmed felt hats or fur hats of their Polish or Hungarian forebears and speak Yiddish among themselves. Both men and boys have long dangling earlocks (*payos*). Girls and women dress extremely modestly, with long dresses with long sleeves. Married women always cover their hair with long scarves or wigs (*sheitels*) and sometimes with a hat over the wig. Men and women are usually segregated, as are children, with boys and girls attending separate schools in the private school systems that all Chassidic groups run.

Some Chassidim work as diamond cutters or merchants in New York's diamond district. Others are business-oriented and deal in computers or electronics, and many are in the garment industry. Their old-world outfits should not fool you into thinking they are not proficient in modern business methods.

There are many different Chassidic groups. They observe many customs and have large families. Each group has its own leader, or rebbe, whose word reigns supreme. One group, Lubavitch (also known as *Chabad*), sends envoys to live in Jewish communities all over the world to influence those communities to become more observant.

Outside of their centers in New York, where each group clusters around its rebbe, and Israel, particularly Jerusalem and Bnai Brak, Chassidim are found in small pockets in most large Jewish communities around the world.

NON-CHASSIDIC JEWS

The non-Chassidic Orthodox are not marked by such distinctive dress. Some men favor dark suits, white shirts, and black hats, while others dress in much the same style as other Americans, but top it off with knitted yarmulkes. Many Orthodox married women cover their hair with *sheitels* (wigs) or hats.

Many non-Chassidic Orthodox men and women attend college or university to qualify for professions, but all place a major emphasis on Torah study and religious activity. The major centers of intensive Orthodox religious education are famous post-high school yeshivoth, located in cities including New York, Baltimore, Cleveland, Chicago, and Lakewood, New Jersey. Some of these institutions bear the same names and are direct descendants of European yeshivoth that were destroyed during the Holocaust but rebuilt on American shores by survivors. Some also have branches in Israel, where it is very common for American *bochurim* (young unmarried male students) to spend a year or more advancing their religious studies. In recent years, a growing number of Orthodox girls spend a post-high school year studying in women-only religious seminaries, often in Israel.

In summary, there are many kinds of Orthodox Jews. They dress differently, wear different kinds of headgear, follow different customs, and favor different lifestyles. Their common feature is that they all accept the Torah and its laws as the supreme guide to the way they lead their lives.

To me, to say one person is more Orthodox than another is a judgment only God can make. The absolute definition of a truly Orthodox person includes the way he or she respects all other people as well as his or her religious observance toward God. It is actions and not just dress that determine one's religiosity. Here, as in any area of life, stereotyping is shallow and misleading.

Shabbos—The Sabbath

WHAT IS *SHABBOS*?

It took God six days to create everything in the heavens and on the earth, and on the seventh He rested. God did not need that seventh day of rest because He was tired, but created it as a gift to the Jewish people to teach them the beautiful concept of a day of rest. That day is called *Shabbos*—the Sabbath.

Jews celebrate Shabbos (or *Shabbat*, as the word is pronounced in the modern Hebrew used in Israel) from sundown on Friday evening until after dark on Saturday night. On this holy day of rest, they should refrain from weekday activities that fall into any one of 39 categories of prohibited activities. These 39 categories were all performed in the construction of the Tabernacle that was erected in the 40 years during which the Israelites wandered in the wilderness after the Exodus from Egypt. The

Tabernacle served as the center of religious worship and served as a model for the Holy Temple that was built by King Solomon in Jerusalem hundreds of years later. The 39 categories of forbidden activities, together with a long list of safeguards added by the rabbis, are the basis of the long set of laws of how to observe the Sabbath.

Sabbath Observance

Keeping the Sabbath—or, in Hebrew, being a *shomer Shabbos*—is a key factor in determining whether a Jew is truly Orthodox. It is impossible to list all the complex laws of Sabbath observance in a few pages, so here is a sample of some of the principal activities an Orthodox Jew cannot perform on Shabbos. He or she cannot:

- Drive or ride in a car, bus, or any other motor vehicle.
- Switch on or off any electrical device, including a television, radio, air conditioner, elevator, electronic door, or even a light switch. This prohibition includes battery operated devices.
- Light a fire, stove, oven, or match.
- Cook food or boil water.
- Earn, spend, or even handle money.
- Use a telephone.
- Plant, plow, cut, or tear grass or other plants.
- Carry from a house to the street, or vice versa, any object, including a wallet, a book, or a pair of glasses. It is permitted to go out while wearing glasses or jewelry.
- Write, draw, or paint.

- Build a structure or assemble or repair a machine.
- Tear paper.

This list is just a small sample of the activities forbidden on the Sabbath. Imagine for a moment some typical Shabbos scenes from the life of an Orthodox Jew, as illustrated by my own family.

- We are sitting down at home when we hear the phone ring insistently. We just have to ignore it. Today, technology has made this easier by developing the answering machine. We just leave it on before the Sabbath begins and pick up our messages after Shabbos.
- Our new refrigerator has a light that goes on every time we open the door, and at the same time the motor kicks in automatically. We took care of the light by unscrewing the light bulb, and stopped the motor from switching on whenever the door opens by installing a bypass circuit.
- When we are staying in a hotel over *Shabbos,* we make sure to take a room on a low floor because the elevator is off limits, and we walk up the stairs. It's great exercise. We are not allowed to use electronic locks, so we request a conventional lock for our room. Many buildings have automatic doors that are activated by a motion detector or a switch under the doormat. Both of these are electrical devices whose use is forbidden to us, so we must either find a conventional door or wait until someone else goes into the building and run in quickly behind them so we do not activate the device. As you can see, advance planning is very important when traveling away from

home. It is not easy, but we regard it as a challenge well worth taking, and have always managed to overcome all the obstacles.

My summary of some of the restrictions associated with Sabbath observance may have persuaded you that Orthodox Jews are a bunch of fanatics who subject themselves every week to an awful experience of deprivation from the good things of life. In fact, *Shabbos*, with all of its observances, is not a burden but instead is a wonderful gift that no Orthodox Jew would consider giving up. Why is that? I am sure you are wondering how people can spend every Saturday without television, cooking, car travel, telephone, yard work, shopping, and so on. How do we manage to survive, and exactly what do we find to do for 25 or so hours that is so wonderful?

A TYPICAL *SHABBOS*

Let me describe a typical Shabbos, as it is experienced every Friday night and Saturday. The woman of the house ushers in the Sabbath by lighting candles, a practice introduced by the rabbis thousands of years ago to make sure the house would be well lit, so that Shabbos would be a bright and enjoyable experience for the family. It is a special time for women. After reciting the blessing over the candles, they say a private prayer expressing their own personal wishes for their family. At least two candles are lit, and many women have the custom to light an additional candle for each child in the family.

The Sabbath candles must be lit at least 18 minutes before sundown, although they are often lit an hour or two earlier on long summer afternoons, to extend the Sabbath. At around the same time, men attend a service at the synagogue to welcome the Sabbath. After services, the family congregates for a festive dinner, which is accompanied by Torah study, singing, and family discussion. After dinner, the family gets together with friends, reads, or studies. It is truly a time when the family bonds together.

On Saturday morning, both men and women attend the synagogue, which becomes the focus of social interaction with friends and neighbors. After the services, families celebrating the birth of a new daughter, the Bar Mitzvah of a son, a forthcoming wedding, or some other festive occasion will often invite the congregation to join them at a kiddush, which may be held in the synagogue or at home. The Hebrew word *kiddush* literally means a blessing recited over wine to observe the Sabbath, but in this context it refers to a light repast and time of socializing after that short blessing. The family then returns home to enjoy the main *Shabbos* meal around noon.

Once again, the family spends quality time together, inviting guests and enjoying wonderful food. They sing, analyze the Bible portion read in synagogue that week, discuss the rabbi's sermon, and report on any interesting people they met in shul (synagogue) that morning. After the lengthy meal, they take a stroll, enjoy a nap, visit friends, study the Bible or Talmud, take part in youth groups, or just spend time together for the rest of the day.

In the late afternoon, men return to the synagogue for the brief afternoon prayer service and then enjoy a light meal and sing, study, and socialize until the evening service is held as the stars come out and the Sabbath ends, early in the winter and late in the summer.

When they return home, it is time to say good-bye to *Shabbos* with the havdalah service. Just as the Sabbath ritual observance began with lighting candles and a prayer over wine, so does it end. The man of the household recites a blessing over a goblet of wine, while another member of the family holds a lit braided candle. He recites another blessing over a container of fragrant spices, whose sweet smell is intended to cheer the soul, which deeply feels the loss of the special Sabbath holiness. After pronouncing a blessing over the candle, which shows that it is now permitted to use fire again, he says one more short blessing to mark the distinction between the Sabbath and weekdays, and it's time to return to normal weekday life. Those present wish each other a good week, and are then off to the pizza shop, theater, concert, or other leisure activity, and then back to the start of a new work week. They were not able to earn any money on the Sabbath, but the good news is that they could not spend any either.

Shabbos is a very special time for Orthodox Jews. It renews and invigorates them for the coming week. It strengthens their family bonds and lets them escape from workaday life and enjoy a beautiful experience for 25 hours every week. It is truly a gift given to us by our Creator.

DEALING WITH SABBATH PROHIBITIONS

Although we cannot do many everyday activities on Shabbos, there are permissible ways to accomplish everything we need to do to make the day an enjoyable experience, rather than one of gloom and restriction. We cannot turn on lights ourselves on the Sabbath, but we can use devices such as thermostats or timers to control lighting and other electrical appliances. These devices must be set before the Sabbath begins so they operate automatically during the Sabbath. We cannot cook, light a match, or turn on a stove, but we can keep precooked food warm in a crock pot, on a hot plate, or over a covered low flame on the stove top, as long as the appliance was on before the commencement of the Sabbath. We can keep a hot water urn on over the whole Shabbos so that we can enjoy a hot cup of tea or coffee whenever we feel like it. And, of course, we can always enjoy a variety of cooked foods that can be eaten cold. In fact, Shabbos meals often provide the finest gourmet experience of the whole week. The day itself, like our delicious Shabbos food, is not an exercise in restriction but an experience out of this world.

THE *ERUV*

One of the most far-reaching prohibitions of Shabbos is that of carrying objects between the home and the street (and also of carrying objects in the street). This means, for example, that it is forbidden even to carry a house key or to wheel a baby carriage in the street. However, it is permissible to do so within the home or in any private domain, such as an enclosed porch or a fenced-in area. Jewish law defines a private domain not as an area owned by a particular person, but as an area that has a fence around it, and this technicality provides a way to overcome many of the problems caused by the prohibition on carrying objects in a public domain.

The ingenious solution that makes it permissible for Orthodox Jews to carry things in the streets around their homes is to transform the public streets into a private domain by constructing an enclosure around the whole neighborhood. It is obviously impractical to build a solid fence around the area, but Jewish law is satisfied by a symbolic fence, which can be made up very inconspicuously by wires and poles to "enclose" parts of the boundary that are not surrounded by real walls. Of course, permission has to be granted by the telephone company, other alterations and some minor construction activity have to be carried out, and the city authorities have to give their permission. This arrangement is called an *eruv*.

Such *eruvs* can be found in parts of many cities in the United States that have significant Orthodox populations, including Baltimore, Chicago, Cleveland, Denver, Detroit, Los Angeles, Miami, New York, St. Louis, and Silver Spring, a Washington, D.C., suburb. Because the exact details of what constitutes a kosher *eruv* are highly technical and involve very complex areas of Jewish law, it takes a considerable time to actually put one into service. In Baltimore, for example, in addition to thousands of hours of volunteer work, it took over five years of meetings, inspections, and construction work before the city's *eruv* was completed and ready for use.

The *eruv* generally surrounds only a small portion of the whole city. Most Orthodox Jews live close to each other, for reasons including the need to be able to walk to a synagogue on the Sabbath, when driving is forbidden, and the desire to be close to kosher food stores and other establishments that serve Orthodox religious needs.

An *eruv* takes care of the problems of house keys and baby carriages, but it should not be considered as providing a license to carry anything on Shabbos. Some items, such as money and objects used for workday activities, may not be carried at all, even inside the house. Others are used for activities that are not compatible with the spirit of Shabbos. For example, I have always told my children that the *eruv* was not put up to allow them to play ball in the street.

It is generally accepted that a preset electronic timer may be used to switch the house lights on and off on Shabbos. However, it would violate the spirit of Shabbos to use the same timer to switch on the television, even for such a compelling need as watching the seventh game of the World Series. Common sense needs to be used, as well as a sensitivity to the meaning of the day.

BUSINESS

Businesses owned by Orthodox Jews are not allowed to operate on the Sabbath, and must be closed from sundown on Friday night until nightfall on Saturday night. If an Orthodox Jew owns a business in partnership with a non-Jew, it may be possible to make an arrangement acceptable to Jewish religious law that permits the business to operate on the Sabbath. The technical details of such an arrangement are highly complex, and a rabbi must be consulted to ensure the acceptability of the partnership agreement and the allocation of profits from Sabbath operations. Saturday is a very important business day for most retail operations in America, and many Orthodox Jews prefer to avoid retail businesses, whether as owners or employees, choosing to go into wholesale ventures instead, because these usually do not operate on Saturdays.

Orthodox professionals cannot conduct any business-related activities on the Sabbath or holidays. Physicians are permitted to provide necessary care for their seriously ill patients on the Sabbath, but must be careful that they follow the technical provisions of halacha (Jewish religious law) in their Sabbath medical activities.

EMERGENCY SITUATIONS

In the case of an emergency situation, such as a life-threatening sickness or other physical danger, the Sabbath prohibitions are voided, because, as the Talmud says, Shabbos was given to the Jewish people to live by, not to die by. It is permissible to dial 911, to drive a seriously sick or injured person to the hospital, or to perform other normally forbidden actions to deal with a life-threatening situation. An Orthodox physician may carry out necessary medical work and even drive on the Sabbath when required. In the absence of an emergency, however, a rabbi should be consulted first to determine the correct way to proceed, because Shabbos is one of the basic institutions of Judaism and must always be taken extremely seriously.

I hope this sketch has given you some insight into the way Orthodox Jews spend Shabbos and what it means to them. You should now understand that when an Orthodox Jew tells you that he or she cannot come to work on Saturday and must leave early on Friday afternoon, it does not reflect an aversion to hard work. The entire concept of Shabbos, and the lifestyle practiced on that day, represents a withdrawal from everyday life into a different sphere of spiritual activity. It is a wonderful world of holiness that has been cherished and preserved for thousands of years, and today's Orthodox Jews are continuing the tradition of their forebears and passing it on to future generations.

Holidays

Orthodox Jews celebrate many holidays during the course of the year. They are very meticulous about observing the religious laws and customs of each one, whether it is a major or a minor festival, whether it is a happy or sad commemoration, and whether the observance involves feasting or fasting.

SKETCHES OF THE JEWISH HOLIDAYS

Rosh Hashana

Rosh Hashana is a two-day festival that celebrates the beginning of the new Jewish year. (1995-96 corresponds to the Jewish year 5756.) It is observed with solemn prayer services and abstinence from work. The distinguishing feature between the Sabbath and Jewish festivals is that on the festival days cooking, some other food preparation activities, and carrying objects in the street are permitted. On the first day of Rosh Hashana (unless it falls on the Sabbath), Orthodox Jews go to the closest river or other body of flowing water to recite special prayers. Rosh Hashana, also known as the Day of Judgment, also marks the beginning of a ten-day period of penitence, ending on Yom Kippur. Rosh Hashana and Yom Kippur are known as the Days of Awe, or High Holidays, the holiest and most serious days of the Jewish calendar. In the secular calendar, these holidays fall in September and/or October.

Yom Kippur

Yom Kippur is a fast that lasts from sundown the previous evening until after dark of the day itself and, unlike every other holiday, has the same full restrictions on work activities that apply on the Sabbath. There are other restrictions on normal activities, including wearing leather shoes; so on this day Orthodox Jews can be seen walking to synagogue in their holiday clothes and wearing sneakers or cloth shoes. The Torah calls Yom Kippur the Sabbath of Sabbaths, and the entire day is spent in the synagogue, praying. Yom Kippur is the holiest day of the year. In the secular calendar, Yom Kippur falls in September or October.

Sukkos

Sukkos begins five days after Yom Kippur. This festive seven-day holiday is followed immediately by two more holidays called *Shemini Atzeres* and *Simchas Torah*. The word *sukkos* refers to huts made of wood, canvas, or plastic, with roofs made of branches or bamboo, which can be seen adjoining homes in Jewish neighborhoods. During Sukkos, Orthodox Jews eat (and sometimes sleep) in these huts to commemorate the way their ancestors lived in the desert for 40 years after the Exodus from Egypt. If it rains, they leave the sukkah and eat inside the house.

The observance of Sukkos serves as a reminder that this world is only a temporary dwelling place, and that the world to come is the true permanent world. Once a year, for seven days, leaving a secure home for a flimsy hut emphasizes the fragility of our existence here on earth. Although sukkas may have rough exteriors, they are decorated beautifully inside. The children of the family participate enthusiastically in building and decorating the sukkah. Sukkah building is a wonderful family project.

Another major observance of Sukkos is the taking of the Four Species during the daily prayer services. This involves shaking a palm stalk (*lulav*), a citron (*esrog*—a citrus fruit resembling a lemon), three myrtle twigs (*hadassim*), and two willow branches (*aravos*). During the week of Sukkos, except on the Sabbath, Orthodox men can be seen in the streets carrying their palm branches to the synagogue.

Work is forbidden on the first two days of Sukkos (*Yom Tov*, literally translated as "good day"). Work necessary for enjoyment of the holiday or to avoid a loss of income is permitted on the interim five days (except, of course, for the Sabbath), which are known as *chol hamoed*— "weekdays of the festival," and most people go to work on these days. Work is forbidden once again on the eighth (Shemini Atzeres) and ninth (Simchas Torah—"rejoicing of the Torah") days. The last day marks the completion of the yearly cycle of reading the entire Torah and is the most joyful of all the Jewish holidays. The synagogue service is extended for hours as men dance around carrying all of the Torah scrolls, and children join in the festivities, dancing, carrying ornate flags, and enjoying candy and sweets.

Passover

Passover (*Pesach*) is an eight-day festival in the spring that commemorates the redemption of the Jewish people from slavery under the Egyptian Pharaoh about 3,300 years ago. The Jews left Egypt in such haste they had no time to allow the bread they took with them to rise, so the event is commemorated by eating the flatbread called *matzoh*. During the eight-day period (actually, from midmorning of the day before the first day of Passover), Jews are forbidden to eat, use, and even own *chometz*, meaning any product that contains wheat, barley, oats, rye, or spelt that has been allowed to rise or ferment. Rising and fermenting are defined as being in contact with water for more than 18 minutes before baking.

Today, companies including Manischewitz, Streits, Rokeach, Haddar, Season, Festive, and Kinneret produce complete lines of kosher-for-Passover foods that are manufactured under rabbinical supervision and guaranteed to contain no leavened ingredients. These foods, from macaroons and pancakes to noodles—and even cakes and rolls—are baked with matzo meal (finely ground matzoh) instead of flour. These products can be found on supermarket shelves in kosher-for-Passover sections throughout America.

The central feature of each of the first two nights of Passover is the *seder* (except in Israel, where only one seder is held). This is an elaborate meal at a magnificently-set table, which accompanies the retelling of the story of the Exodus of the Jews from slavery in Egypt. The seder is designed to instruct the children and keep their attention. It involves many beautiful customs, songs, elaborate discussions, and traditional rituals that help the participants actually relive the experience of slavery and the Exodus to freedom. It is not uncommon for a seder to take four, five, or even six hours.

Work is forbidden on the first two and last two days of Passover, but those work activities necessary for enjoyment of the holiday or to avoid financial loss are permitted during the intermediate four days of *chol hamoed* (except, of course, on the Sabbath). Passover falls in March and/or April.

Shavuos

Exactly 49 days (seven weeks) after the second day of Passover comes the holiday of Shavuos (Pentecost, or the Feast of Weeks). This is perhaps the Jewish holiday that is least known and recognized by non-Jews and the least practiced by nonobservant Jews. At the time when the Temple stood in Jerusalem, Shavuos was celebrated by the bringing of the first produce from the new harvest of wheat and other crops, but today its main significance is that it marks the anniversary of God's giving of the Torah to Moses on Mount Sinai. To commemorate this central event of Jewish history, after the first evening meal at the beginning of the holiday, many men and boys return to the synagogue and spend the entire night studying Torah until dawn breaks and the morning prayer service begins. Work (except for cooking, some other types of food preparation, and carrying objects outside) is forbidden on both days of Shavuos. Dairy foods and cheesecake are the traditional holiday specialties. Shavuos usually falls in June.

These are the major Jewish holidays. There are also several minor holidays and fasts. The main ones are Purim and Chanukah.

Purim

Purim celebrates the miraculous escape of Jews living in the Persian Empire from the annihilation plotted by their foe, Haman. This deliverance came as a result of the efforts and prayers of Queen Esther, who was Jewish, and her uncle and spiritual guide, Mordechai. Their leadership inspired the whole Jewish people to repent. Purim is celebrated by public reading of the Book of Esther (the *Megillah*), exchange of presents of food, feasting and drinking wine, and children dressing up in holiday costume. On the secular calendar, Purim falls in late February or March.

Chanukah

Chanukah celebrates the victory of the Maccabees over the Syrian-Greek occupying army. The major observance is the ceremonial lighting in the home and synagogue of the Chanukah menorah (a straight candelabrum with eight branches). On the first night of the holiday, one candle is lit, and an additional candle is lit each successive night, until all eight are lit. Special prayers are also recited each day of Chanukah, and special foods, such as *latkes* (potato pancakes), are eaten. A four-sided spinning top, or dreidel, is a special holiday game. Chanukah falls in December.

Tisha B'Av

Tisha B'Av is a day of mourning for the destruction of both Temples in Jerusalem and other national Jewish tragedies that occurred on the same date of the Jewish calendar. It is observed by a fast lasting from sundown the previous evening until nightfall of the day itself, reading of the Book of Lamentations, and recitation of many *kinnot*, or mourning elegies. Tisha B'Av falls in July or August.

Every Jewish holiday has its own particular religious laws and customs based on the Torah and rabbinical authorities. The order of the day always involves performing religious rituals and customs, eating traditional foods, wearing proper holiday dress, and enjoying family togetherness.

Restrictions on Work During Holidays

During the major holidays, either for the whole period or some part of it, work is forbidden. The restrictions on work are almost the same as those on the Sabbath, except that cooking food and carrying objects in the street are permitted. The single exception is the holy day of Yom Kippur, when all of the Sabbath restrictions apply.

Passover and Sukkos extend for eight and nine days, respectively, and both begin and end with two work-forbidden days (Yom Tov). The days in between are known as *chol hamoed*, or intermediate days. On these days, special holiday prayers are recited, and other holiday ritual observances are practiced, but necessary work is permitted.

On the minor holidays and fast days (when no eating or drinking is allowed), Orthodox Jews may work.

The following table lists the major holidays observed during each calendar year, how many days each holiday lasts, and the number of days Orthodox Jews are required to be absent from work.

Name of Major Holiday (Yom Tov)	Duration of Holiday (Days)	Number of Days Work is Forbidden
Rosh Hashana (Jewish New Year)	2	2
Yom Kippur (Day of Atonement)	1	1
Sukkos (Tabernacles)	7*	2*
Shemini Atzeres, Simchas Torah (follows Sukkos immediately)	2*	2*
Pesach (Passover)	8*	4*
Shavuos (Pentecost or Feast of Weeks)	2*	2*
Total Days	22	13

*Outside of Israel. In Israel, each of these numbers should be reduced by 1, except for Passover, when the number of work-forbidden days should be reduced by 2. The number of days celebrated in Israel corresponds to the commandment found in the Torah. Celebrating the extra days outside of Israel is an ancient custom dating back thousands of years to the era when people outside of Israel were not able to be sure of the exact day when the holiday started.

The table shows that there are a maximum total of 13 holidays during the year when Orthodox Jews are forbidden to work, but some of those days fall on a Saturday or Sunday. This means that the number of weekdays when they cannot report for work is actually somewhere between six and eleven. In addition to this, the early sunset during winter means they must leave work on Friday afternoons early enough to arrive home in time to prepare for Shabbos.

Orthodox Jews make up the missed work time in various ways, including working on Sundays, coming in early on Fridays or leaving late on other days, and working on legal or non-Jewish religious holidays. Some may choose to take the entire week of the major holidays as their annual vacation so that they do not have to come in to work on the intermediate days (*chol hamoed*). Some may take single vacation days off on minor holidays or fast days. Most Orthodox Jews have a powerful work ethic and are highly productive. In general, if employers understand the religious restrictions of Orthodox Jews and allow the individual employee's performance to speak for itself, they will probably be gratified by the results.

Orthodox Jewish Celebrations

GENERAL REMARKS ON DRESS AND BEHAVIOR

In all Orthodox Jewish ceremonies and celebrations, appropriate modest dress is required. It is inappropriate for women to wear slacks or sleeveless or low-cut gowns. In Orthodox synagogues and at some functions, men and women sit separately. In synagogues, women often sit in a balcony or in a section behind a separator (*mechitzah*), the height and appearance of which varies according to the custom of the community. Jewish men are expected to have their heads covered with a *yarmulke*, hat, or other covering. Non-Jews are not required or expected to cover their heads, but most may feel more comfortable and less conspicuous if they wear a *yarmulke*.

Generally speaking, adhering to modest dress and using common sense will make you feel comfortable at Orthodox religious events.

BRIS (CIRCUMCISION)

The circumcision of Jewish boys on the eighth day following their birth is a covenant between God and the Jewish people that was established at the time of the patriarch Abraham, the first Jew. The *bris* (which in full is actually called a *bris milah*—covenant of circumcision) symbolizes the baby's entering this covenant, even though every baby born of a Jewish mother is automatically Jewish.

The ceremony may take place in a home, synagogue, hospital, or any other environment where it can be carried out safely on an eight-day-old baby. The learned and skilled man who carries it out is called a *mohel*. The *bris* itself is followed by a meal to celebrate the occasion, a custom that also dates back to Abraham.

If the *mohel* or a doctor determines that performing the operation on the eighth day would be dangerous in any way to the child, the *bris* is postponed until the baby is well enough that the circumcision can be performed safely.

BAR MITZVAH AND BAT MITZVAH (OR BAS MITZVAH)

According to Jewish religious law, when a boy becomes 13 years old, or a girl becomes 12, they are no longer considered children, but full-fledged Jews responsible for their actions. This stage in life is referred to as becoming Bar Mitzvah (for boys) or Bas Mitzvah (for girls). Literally, the words mean *a son or daughter of the commandments*. In America today, this simple automatic passage has been commercialized by caterers and merchants, who have turned the event into a food and gift extravaganza—and the kids love it!

The true importance to a child of the Bar Mitzvah or Bas Mitzvah is that he or she has been educated to become aware that he or she is now a responsible Jewish adolescent, charged with the many duties of a Jewish adult. For boys, the most obvious example is that they now begin to wear *tefillin* (phylacteries). These are two small black leather boxes containing biblical verses that are strapped on the arm and around the head and worn every weekday while saying the morning prayers.

The actual occasion of the Bar Mitzvah is usually marked by the Bar Mitzvah boy reading part or all of the weekly portion of the Torah in the synagogue during the Sabbath (and/or weekday) service after (or on) his thirteenth birthday. Usually the boy (and sometimes the girl) prepares a speech or study project on a Torah subject to be given on the day of the Bar Mitzvah or Bas Mitzvah, at a special festive meal. Sometimes the celebration develops into an elaborate party, but there is no religious requirement to go overboard. The child becomes obligated in adult religious observances even if there is no celebration at all.

COURTSHIP AND THE MARRIAGE PROCESS

When a prudent consumer is about to purchase an appliance or automobile, the buyer educates him/herself as to the reliability and reputation of the name brand he/she is considering to acquire. Hours of research, studying "consumer reports", and getting recommendations from friends or other due diligence are all quite common. Only after thorough study and accurate research will the buyer feel confident about his/her product choice and decide which brand to purchase.

Too often in our culture young adults develop a relationship with a person that they have little knowledge about. It is only after they begin dating that they learn of each others' past reputation, personality traits and family backgrounds. The danger with this is that judgments can often be clouded when people have already developed a social relationship, where emotions and feelings can get in the way of sound judgment and astute common sense.

In many orthodox circles the research on a prospective dating partner is done well in advance of the first date. This research involves personal references, a detailed profile of the person's character and family history, and recommendations from respected persons who have a thorough knowledge of character, and personality, religious and social aspects pertaining to the individual under consideration. This detailed research of character analysis and eventual recommendations by reliable sources is known as the *shidduch* process.

The Shidduch:

Very often, Orthodox young men and women of marriageable age are introduced to one another by mutual friends, rabbis, or some other third party acquaintance. The person who makes the suggestion or recommends this match is known as the *shadchin*. This introduction or suggestion that two people get to know each other and then begin dating is a wonderful way for two serious marriage minded partners to meet one another.

The first recorded practice of the *shidduch* process dates back to the Bible, when Abraham asked his loyal trusted servant, *Eliezer*, to seek out the land and find a most suitable wife for his most cherished son *Isaac*. His choice was based on *Rivkah's* exemplary character traits and compassionate actions towards both him and his herd of animals. Recognizing in *Rivkah* her concern for mankind as well as her concern for animals, *Eliezer* realized she would be an excellent match for *Isaac*.

So to, today, a person who suggests or recommends that two people begin to enter into a dating relationship should do so with a thorough knowledge of the character, reputation, and family background of the two parties. After each party is comfortable with the proposed prospect and feels that a good possibility exists that the other party would be a suitable marriage prospect, a first date or meeting is arranged.

After this introduction or first date, the young adults make their own determination as to their continued courtship. This is truly an excellent way for young marriageable prospects to meet. *Shidduchim* make a great deal of common sense because individuals are paired based on similarities of culture, life style, religious beliefs, character, and personality traits. The *shidduch* process is an excellent insurance policy, so that before two people get involved with each other, each party has full disclosure of the other party's past. Naturally, credibility of all information and details depends on the credibility of the sources and accuracy of the information obtained.

The *shidduch* process is preferred by many orthodox young adults because it is a serious approach that has proven to have been a successful method of matchmaking. Modern day computer matching services are based on the same principles of good old fashion matchmaking, matching similarities and commonalities of two prospective clients.

While many orthodox people meet on their own whether it be socially, in college, or through other community activities, there is another definite advantage to the *shidduch* process. People from distant communities can be introduced to one another, who otherwise would never have had the opportunity to meet. For an interesting prospect a suitor can go from New York to Los Angeles or even oversees if the prospect is promising. This gives a serious marriageable candidate a world wide spectrum of excellent prospects to choose from, when considering a marriage partner.

The stereotype of prearranged marriages where there is no freedom of choice between bride and groom is a misconception. A prearranged marriage where bride and groom meet under the canopy is extremely rare and is only practiced by a small group of ultra orthodox Chassidic sects. In these very infrequent prearranged marriages, the families of the bride and groom usually enter into some kind of an agreement, but even here the young adults are hopefully part of the decision making process at some point.

Orthodox Jewish couples have an excellent record of successful, happy marriages. While divorce rates are spiraling in America, Orthodox marriages have a very low percentage of breakup when compared to society as a whole. I attribute much of this success to the beautiful religious laws of the Orthodox Jewish marriage, as well as to the Orthodox lifestyle, and to the whole system of the *shidduch* process.

WEDDINGS

A Jewish wedding is a festive, lively, and beautiful occasion. It is customary that the bride and groom do not see each other for a week before the wedding. On the day of the wedding, the bride and groom fast until the ceremony. They recite the same confessional prayer said on Yom Kippur, the holiest day of the year. They thus begin their new life in a state of spiritual purity.

At the wedding hall, after the guests have begun to arrive and socialize, the groom signs the formal marriage contract, and the proceedings get under way. The bridegroom walks slowly to the hall where the bride is sitting. He is escorted by his father and the bride's father and accompanied by most of the men present, while his friends sing and dance in front of him. When he reaches the bride, who is seated on a throne-like chair, he drops the veil over her face in a ceremony called *badeken* (veiling). At this time, the bride is blessed by her father and prominent rabbis who may be present.

The guests now proceed to wait for the wedding ceremony, or *chuppah*. At Orthodox weddings, men and women sit separately during the ceremony, and, although customs vary, they sometimes sit at separate tables during the wedding banquet as well. There are separate dance floors for men and women, and there may be a divider (*mechitza*) down the center of the hall, with men on one side and women on the other.

Although the word *chuppah* is used to refer to the wedding ceremony, its literal meaning is a structure consisting of four poles holding up a canopy of fabric, often decorated with flowers, under which the bride (*kallah*) and groom (*chasan*) stand during the ceremony. It symbolizes the home the couple will now begin to build together.

The groom comes down the aisle to the *chuppah* first, escorted by his parents (or sometimes by his father and the bride's father) and waits for the bride, who walks down the aisle with her parents (or sometimes the two mothers). The bride walks around the groom seven times, with her mother and his mother walking behind her, carrying her bridal train. Then the officiating rabbi recites a blessing over a cup of wine and another blessing to declare the couple man and wife. The groom slips the ring on the bride's finger and declares her his wife, and the couple drink from the wine. The wedding contract is then read in Aramaic, an ancient language related to Hebrew, and seven more blessings are recited, often by different rabbis or by relatives or other people the bride and groom want to honor. Another cup of wine is drunk, and the ceremony is concluded when the groom breaks a glass by stamping on it. The breaking of the glass is a ceremony introduced thousands of years ago to commemorate the destruction of the Temple, informing the people present that Jews are required even at the most joyful times to remember this historic tragedy and the plight of the Jewish people in exile.

After the breaking of the glass, everyone present calls out *"Mazal Tov!"* (Good luck!), and the new couple walks together back up the aisle they had earlier come down separately, while everyone present congratulates them and their families. The bride and groom go together to a closed room, where they enjoy their first few private minutes together as man and wife, and break their fast. When they emerge a short while later, it provides the photographer his first opportunity to take pictures of the couple together. Taking photographs of the couple by themselves and with their relatives is usually a lengthy procedure. This often means that the bride and groom are not able to greet the guests for quite a long time. When they finally come out from the photograph session, the band strikes up an overture, and the festive dancing begins. The guests, hopefully, have already partaken of the first courses of the wedding feast, and they greet the new couple with joyful singing and vigorous dancing, as the couple is introduced as husband and wife.

If you are fortunate enough to attend such a wedding, don't just watch; jump in and have a good time. Not only is it good aerobic exercise for your body, but the overwhelming spirit of joy will be good for your soul.

FUNERALS

Accompanying a deceased Jew to his or her final resting place is one of the greatest mitzvos (religious obligations) a Jew can perform. The deceased must be buried (not cremated) wearing simple white shrouds in a plain pine box, not an elaborate coffin. The burial is held as soon as possible, on the day of death or the next day, depending on how long it takes to make funeral arrangements and how much travel time is needed by relatives who live far away. Embalming is forbidden, the body must not be in open view, and no floral or other decorations are used. These customs all express the strong Jewish tradition that shuns all forms of ostentation during mourning. The funeral service generally encompasses one or more eulogies (*hespedim*) praising the deceased, except on certain holidays, when eulogies are not permitted. Psalms and a memorial prayer are also recited. Following the funeral service, the casket is taken to a cemetery for burial. There, other prayers, including the kaddish, are recited by the gravesite.

Following the burial, the immediate relatives of the deceased return home to begin a seven-day mourning period (*shivah*). Except on the Sabbath, the mourners sit on low chairs to symbolize their mourning. Mourners also demonstrate the loss they have suffered by wearing a jacket or shirt that has been torn, symbolizing the life that was torn away, and by not wearing leather shoes. It is also customary to cover the mirrors in a house of mourning. Friends visit the mourners to pay their respects, and three daily prayer services (morning, afternoon, and night) are held in the house during the *shivah*.

A less-intense period of mourning, with fewer restrictions, continues for a full year for people who have lost a parent, and for one month for those who have lost a spouse, a sibling, or a child. Those in mourning for a parent recite the kaddish at each of the three daily prayer services for the whole year, or more precisely, for eleven months.

It is appropriate for visitors to a *shivah* house to make donations to charity, and kosher food platters are acceptable, as are kosher pastries, fruit baskets, or other kosher prepared food items, because food preparation is forbidden by the mourners during *shivah*. Flowers are not appropriate.

Everything You Ever Wanted to Know About Keeping Kosher, But Were Afraid to Ask

PORTRAIT OF A KOSHER GOURMET

I am neither an ordained rabbi nor a trained kosher supervisor, but eating strictly kosher is very important to me. I am a practicing Orthodox Jew, following the same tradition observed in my parents' and grandparents' homes. It is a tradition that goes back some 3,300 years, to the time when the kosher laws were first laid down, when the Torah was given to the Jewish people on Mount Sinai. Hundreds of thousands of people share the same kosher preference, and their buying habits are increasingly important to the food industry, both in the United States and globally. Knowing about those habits may also be important to you personally, especially if you have friends, colleagues, or employees who keep kosher. You probably know some people who keep kosher, and if you have ever eaten together with them, you probably have questions about the purposes, principles, and practices of kosher dietary law. I hope to answer some of the more common questions about kosher observance and observers.

FOOD IN JUDAISM

Tradition plays an important role in the food of Judaism. Holidays are celebrated with foods that serve symbolic purposes. Sometimes, particular foods are actually required by the Torah, and sometimes they are eaten as a time-honored custom.

- On Passover, the Torah commands us to eat *matzoh* (crisp flatbread crackers) recalling the Jews' hasty flight from slavery in Egypt and the unrisen bread they took with them, and *maror* (bitter herbs), symbolizing the bitterness of slavery in Egypt.
- On Rosh Hashana (the Jewish New Year) Jews dip a sweet apple into honey to symbolize hope for a sweet and joyous year.
- On Shavuos, Jews celebrate the receiving of the Torah with luscious cheesecake. This, as well as other special holiday treats like blintzes, is a dairy food. Shavuos is the only holiday on which milk-based foods are featured. This custom arose because milk is the food enjoyed by a newborn baby. It is an appropriate symbol for a newborn nation, which the Children of Israel became at Mount Sinai, when God gave them the Torah.
- Our Sabbath table is graced at three meals with luscious braided *challahs* (bread loaves) that remind

us of the Temple service of thousands of years ago, and during the day we enjoy a delicious *cholent* stew based on potatoes, beans, and meat (or other variations) that has been cooking on the stove since Friday afternoon. *Cholent* is one of the most authentic of all Jewish dishes. It fills the need for a hot food that can be eaten during the day without transgressing the prohibition of putting food on the stove on the Sabbath itself. Different Jewish communities all over the world have their own unique versions, with varying ingredients reflecting the local cuisine.

There are also religious and symbolic meanings behind other traditional Jewish foods, such as bagels and lox and *kugels*. Few people know where these tasty treats came from, but who cares? It's our tradition, and they are mouthwatering delicacies that help us celebrate our festivities.

Driving my interest in food was the fact that I *love* to eat—in fact, food has been my profession for over 25 years. As a master of the culinary arts, I make a terrific salad and pride myself on my barbecue and cooking techniques. In addition, I have acquired a quarter-century of specialty gourmet food training in the role of CEO of a major gourmet food (nonkosher) distributor in the mid-Atlantic states. I have frequently served as a consultant, lecturer, and panelist in food symposia in the United States and abroad.

My training goes back a long way. Starting when I was a young boy, my father, the owner of a gourmet food business, introduced me to that world, "*shlepping*" me around Washington to fine French restaurants such as Jean Pierre, Lion d'Or, Chez Francois, and La Nicoise, and to Georgetown food palaces and boutiques such as La

Cheeserie, Wine and Cheese, the Georgetown Coffee House, and The French Market. During these tantalizing trips I was always looking, smelling, yearning, but never really tasting. I was introduced to Wally Amos of Famous Amos, and while others tasted, I listened, and yearned, as Wally described the taste and texture of his original chocolate chip cookie.

The years went by, our family company grew, and as CEO I became like a blind man whose other faculties had to offset his lack of vision. I learned to use my other senses to compensate for not tasting nonkosher food. I used vision, smell, touch, and even hearing to experience the food I could not eat. I became an expert on Beluga caviar, although my tongue never touched it. I became a connoisseur of nonalcoholic champagne and sparkling juices, able to judge the beverage by its bubbly effervescence and bouquet. I became an authority on escargots, by observing their texture and the way they were garnished with garlic and butter to season them perfectly. I was able to do these things without tasting because I experienced the culinary arts with every other sense.

In case you are skeptical that all of that yearning and self-education qualified me as an expert, I must mention the additional undisputed fact that those around me, my wonderful mom and my beautiful wife, may be the two greatest kosher chefs the world has known, so that I do have actual hands-on eating experience, using conventional tasting as my basic criterion, of good old-fashioned home-style cooking.

My roster of acquaintances has included Cajun genius Paul Prudhomme and Tex-Mex virtuoso Dan Jardine. I have advised master chef Dominique D'Ermo, creator of the famous U.S. Senate bean soup, sipped tea with the likes of Sam Twining, and even once found myself standing right next to Julia Child. Living in my two worlds, I have become a self-proclaimed expert on kosher gourmet food. Paul Prudhomme and I once discussed the possibilities of New York's first kosher Cajun eatery, and the son of Wick Fowler of Two Alarm Chili told me about the rabbis who visited Texas to inspect his cooking kettle to confirm that his fiery fare answered to a Higher Authority. Would you believe that even the masterful French chef Dominique asked me for my grandmother's chicken soup recipe?

Although I hold no formal culinary diploma, I can point to a mountain of experience and a somewhat smaller middle-age bulge to prove my case. I earned my qualifications the hard way—I ate whatever I could. And I continue to enjoy fine dining and delightful culinary experiences.

WHO ELSE EATS KOSHER . . . AND WHAT IS KOSHER?

Orthodox Jews always eat strictly kosher food. But, for a variety of reasons, others now actively seek out kosher products. These people include Moslems, Seventh Day Adventists, vegetarians, people with dairy allergies, and members of the general public. Although not all kosher foods are particularly healthy, many items on the market that bear kosher certification are perceived as healthy because they generally contain no animal fats. Perception means a great deal, and consumer perceptions have made kosher a hot concept in the 1990s. This trend is putting more kosher items on supermarket shelves as manufacturers seek to expand their share of the consumer market by gaining kosher certification.

More kosher products on grocery shelves has meant more tasting and less yearning for people such as me. As an observant Jew, I know I can only frequent kosher restaurants and fast food eateries that operate under strict kosher supervision. Growing up as a kid in the 1960s, I often felt a yearning as I walked past a MacDonalds (Wow, what would it be like to have a Big Mac?), Pizza Hut (Umm . . . cheese and pepperoni topping), Dunkin' Donuts, or a Chinese carry-out and wondered what it would be like to be able to partake of all the culinary experiences of the fast food world. Would I ever get to taste the Whopper? But today, those experiences are much less remote.

Certain cities pose few problems for the kosher epicure. New York, Los Angeles, Chicago, Cleveland, Baltimore, and other metropolitan areas that have large populations of Orthodox Jews have a diverse array of kosher eating establishments. These include MacDonalds look-alikes, serving all-beef patties; pizza shops; Chinese, Italian, Japanese, French, and other specialized restaurants; and even kosher Dunkin' Donuts franchises. Kosher food operations are opening in many cities in the United States, Canada, Europe, and Israel. Supermarket shelves are stocked with kosher-approved products bearing symbols such as the Ⓤ, the Ⓚ, the 𝕂, the ☆, to name the best-known of the more than 200 registered symbols of kosher supervision agencies.

Kosher food no longer means only gefilte fish, matzoh, and borscht. Today, kosher food includes gourmet pastries, pastas, olive oils, Swiss chocolates, chilies, salsas, chips, and confections, all bearing reliable kosher certification. In recent years, imitation crab, lobster, and bacon strips have given new options to the Jewish palate, but the tofu-topped burger that was supposed to be the next best thing to the cheese Whopper never really made it. For the gourmet kosher cook, virgin olive oil, sun dried tomatoes, Dijon mustard, and even balsamic vinegars with kosher certification are available. Those keeping kosher can satisfy their taste buds and their religious scruples at the same time with household names like Entenmanns, Carvel, Friendly, Häagen-Dazs, Drake's, Stella D'Oro, Pepperidge Farms, Celestial Teas, M & M's, and even Godiva chocolates. All of these companies are on a rapidly growing world-wide list of companies producing foods under kosher supervision.

This kosher cornucopia is becoming widely available. For example, one large kosher supermarket in Baltimore stocks over 10,000 kosher products. In fact, consumer demand is so high that another kosher supermarket recently opened just four blocks away. In addition, Baltimore boasts many kosher restaurants, including three Dunkin' Donuts outlets, two pizzerias, one Chinese and one Continental restaurant, two superb delis, a Kosher Bite burger, a dairy restaurant, two full-line carry-outs, and four kosher bakeries, all within a two-mile radius. The city also has eight or nine kosher caterers, as well as separate kosher kitchens serving the Sheraton and Hyatt hotels; kosher coffee shops and yogurt shops; kosher eating facilities at colleges, including Johns Hopkins University and the University of Maryland; a hand-made matzoh factory; several candy manufacturers; and even a kosher hot dog stand at Oriole Park at Camden Yards.

Even so, no other place in the world can compete with Israel and New York in offering kosher versions of virtually every imaginable international culinary delight. Israel has a Wendy's, McDonalds, Pizza Hut and Burger King, all franchises of their American counterparts. Some of them are kosher, although the standards of the certifying authorities vary. Even in Israel, you must always check the supervising agency. For the true epicure, kosher establishments in New York can supply pate, venison, sushi, quiches, pastas, ribs, and other gourmet delicacies, accompanied by elaborate wine lists, which offer Bordeaux from France, Italian sparkling wines, fruity California wines, New York State chardonnays, zinfandels, champagnes, and a variety of Israeli gourmet wines. Traditional kosher fare has penetrated the general American diet, so that the old tag line "You don't have to be Jewish" applies in force, as Gentile Americans nosh on bagels and cheesecake throughout the United States. The 1980s was the decade that ushered in such tastes as Thai, Cajun, salsas, and other spicy foods, but the food trends of the 1990s are marked by a healthy lifestyle and low-cholesterol, fat-free, good tasting treats, all features making "kosher" a term desired by consumers seeking wholesome, healthy foods.

DOES KOSHER MEAN THE SAME AS HEALTHY?

Orthodox Jews eat kosher food because it is good for their souls. When it comes to the body, however, it may not be comparably healthy. For example, coconut oil processed in a kosher plant is certainly kosher, but it is just as unhealthy as lard or other animal fats. Kosher hot dogs are all beef, but may contain just as much salt and nitrates as their nonkosher counterparts. Health-conscious consumers need to study the labels on *all* foods to ensure proper standards of nutrition and health.

When purchasing kosher products, the Madison Avenue slogan "We answer to a Higher Authority" must be taken with a grain of salt. The food itself may contain considerably more than a grain of salt, plus cholesterol, saturated fats, additives, and calories that the buyer may not necessarily want to consume. The Higher Authority does not guarantee either the nutritional acceptability or the healthfulness of a product that meets every religious requirement of the kosher laws. As elsewhere, the educated consumer needs to heed the ancient slogan *caveat emptor*—let the buyer beware. Always read the label for all nutritional information.

WHY DO JEWS KEEP KOSHER?

Observant Jews follow the kosher dietary laws because they are commanded to do so by the Torah, which includes the Hebrew Bible (the Old Testament) and its elaboration by rabbinical authorities in the Talmud and later works. The most authoritative compilation of all the applicable laws is the code of Jewish law called the *Shulchan Aruch*. The Torah does not give any explanation for why Jews must keep these laws except that they were given by God, but religious commentators have discussed in philosophic terms some of the effects kosher observance might be expected to have. For example, kosher species include domesticated, vegetarian food-consuming animals such as cows and sheep but not wild animals or predatory birds, suggesting that humans are supposed to live in peace rather than engaging in violence. Similarly, Jews are discouraged from hunting for sport and are forbidden to eat animals that have been killed by shooting. Kosher slaughter insists that animals be killed with extreme care and a minimum of pain. It is the most humane method of slaughter.

Following the kosher laws requires a very high degree of self-control, and kosher observance also fosters social cohesiveness. Observant Jews must eat only in kosher homes or establishments that follow the kosher laws, and much of their shopping must be done in stores where kosher products such as meat and poultry are available. This common kosher concern links observant Jews all over the world and keeps them together, so that individuals traveling in the United States, Europe, or Asia will automatically be drawn to the same kosher establishments.

I think that the best description of the Jewish attitude toward the kosher laws was expressed by the character Tevye in the Broadway show *Fiddler on the Roof*:

> *Tradition! It's God's law, so who are we to question it? Tradition! Tradition!*

I, like Tevye, often lift my eyes up to heaven and ask:

> *Dear God, would it have been so terrible to have allowed us to taste just one Big Mac or just one Oreo cookie, one tiny crab cake or lobster? Just a taste. Dear God, you made many wonderful foods, so what would you say if we tasted those too? Will it change the world? Will it change us? Sha! Tradition! Tradition!*
>
> *But it's not only a tradition—its the Halacha (Jewish Law)*
>
> *And after all, a Big Mac—think of all that cholesterol, and the heartburn. An Oreo, a crab cake, a lobster—who needs it? Dear God, you gave me kishke, cholent, tzimmes, taiglech. Ahh, what the rest of the world is missing. Tradition! Tradition!*

What Makes Food Kosher?

After this excursion into the world of the kosher consumer, it is time to explain exactly what requirements must be met for food to be considered kosher. Kosher is a Hebrew word that means fit or proper. In brief, Jewish religious law lays down three sets of conditions that any food must meet before it is considered fit to be eaten by a Jew, or "kosher."

First, the raw ingredients must be acceptable. Second, they must be combined and prepared in a permissible fashion. Third, they must be placed on kosher utensils and served in an appropriate manner.

The laws governing each of these phases of food preparation are extremely stringent. Kosher food must be produced and prepared in a strictly kosher kitchen or plant in which all of the food and equipment meet all of the applicable kosher requirements. In commercial food preparation, it is often necessary to have a rabbi or *mashgiach* (a religiously qualified supervisor) to oversee the entire process, either present all of the time or periodically visiting the plant to check the ingredients and inspect the processing.

There are many technical regulations specific to each food group, and I will attempt to list some of the more basic rules for each category. I have tried to make the facts in this account as informative as possible. I am discussing them on a fairly general level, so you need to remember that in any real-life encounter with a question of kashruth (the set of rules that determine whether something is kosher), you *must* bring your questions to a qualified rabbinical expert, who will generally ask for a host of specific details, that may at times surprise you.

It is very important to know that Orthodox, Conservative, and Reform Jews differ greatly with respect to their standards in kosher matters, with the Orthodox having the most stringent requirements. Within the Orthodox camp itself, the rabbis who set the rules for different supervisory agencies may differ among themselves on certain technical details. A worldwide survey by *Kashrus Magazine* in November 1995 identified over 200 different kosher supervision agencies (of which more than 100 were in the United States), most with their own trademark symbols to indicate the products they certify. The bewildered manufacturer who wants to increase sales by arranging for kosher certification of the company's products, or the gracious host who wants to provide acceptable kosher-certified food for an observant guest must choose the supervising agency carefully. Many smaller agencies are unknown to many kosher consumers, who are strongly opinionated folks and often simply refuse to buy a product with a *hechsher* (kosher certification) they do not recognize. A useful rule of thumb for me is that any one of the symbols Ⓤ, Ⓚ, 𝕭, and ☆

will be accepted by most Orthodox Jews worldwide. In general terms, each of these four agencies usually accepts products supervised by the other three. This is particularly important when a foodstuff supervised by one agency contains ingredients or products supervised by another. These kosher agencies have a very visible presence and have won a high level of consumer awareness and acceptance. Smaller agencies may be equally reliable but lack national or worldwide consumer acceptance simply because of their limited regional profile. Anyone seeking to serve kosher consumers should first check with a reliable rabbinical authority to ensure proper kosher standards and qualified kosher certification.

What about a plain K? Many products have a plain letter K (which, of course, is the first letter of the word *Kosher*) printed somewhere on the label. It means that the manufacturer claims that the item is kosher, but it may or may not have rabbinical supervision that provides a solid backing to the claim. A single letter K cannot be registered as a trademark; the kosher consumer needs to play detective to find out exactly what the letter means. For example, for the many products produced by Kraft or Kellogg's, there is, in fact, a widely accepted supervisory agency behind the K, but for various reasons the company does not want the agency's trademark symbol to appear. In other cases, supervision may be provided by an organization on which few Orthodox consumers would rely. This supervision, sometimes by the owner of the company, may be based on his or her own ideas, which may have little connection with the actual principles of kashruth. Therefore a K is no guarantee of kosher acceptance by Orthodox Jews. Some states have their own laws protecting kosher consumers from products making false claims of kosher status, but Orthodox Jews generally insist on knowing that the products they eat are certified by a Rabbi or an organization they trust.

SOME BASIC RULES OF KASHRUTH

Kosher Species

The first qualification for a foodstuff to be kosher is that it must come from a kosher species. Kosher animals must satisfy two conditions: they must have split hooves and chew their cud. These conditions are satisfied by cattle and sheep as well as more exotic fare such as goats, deer, and similar game animals.

For birds, there is no such simple rule. Common poultry species such as chicken, turkey, duck, and goose are permitted, and birds of prey such as hawk and eagle are forbidden. There are some technical indicators as to whether a species is forbidden, but the operative rule is that a particular kind of bird is kosher only when there is a historical tradition that Jews eat it.

Fish are permitted only when they have both fins and scales. Salmon, halibut, trout, carp, rockfish, sardines, and the ever-popular tuna are kosher, whereas catfish, eel, and all shellfish, including oysters, lobsters, crabs, and shrimp, are not. Canned, smoked, and cooked fish, such as tuna and sardines, must be processed only with kosher oils (discussed later) and processed in a plant in which neither the products nor the equipment come into contact with nonkosher foods.

Milk and Eggs

Milk and eggs are permitted only when they come from kosher birds or animals. To prevent Jews from unknowingly consuming milk from nonkosher animals, the rabbis decreed thousands of years ago that a Jew must observe the actual milking process. Milk produced in this approved way is called *cholov yisroel* (literally, Israelite milk). Today, because all milk produced in the United States (although not everywhere else in the world) is closely supervised by government regulators, it is widely accepted that all milk sold commercially in this country is kosher. However, some Orthodox Jews continue the tradition of drinking only *cholov yisroel*.

Cheese

Whether soft or hard, cheese requires kosher certification. Most hard cheeses are produced from milk curdled by rennet, a substance that may be extracted from the stomach of a young calf. Kosher cheeses are processed with kosher-approved enzymes.

KOSHER MEAT: THE LONG ROAD FROM FARM TO FREEZER

Shechitah

The first hurdle a kosher animal or bird has to pass on its long journey to becoming kosher meat is *shechitah* (slaughter), which must be performed in the approved manner by a highly trained and religiously qualified *shochet* (ritual slaughterer). The *shochet* takes care to ensure that the animal is killed instantly and painlessly, which requires the use of a special knife, which he frequently inspects to guarantee that its cutting edge is perfectly sharp. For animals, both the windpipe (trachea) and the foodpipe (esophagus) must be severed, while in the case of fowl, it is sufficient to cut either one of them. After performing the *shechitah*, the *shochet* must examine the cut to make sure it was made correctly. Then he, as well as the *mashgiach* (religious supervisor), checks the animal for lesions, disease, or any of the other imperfections that make the animal *treifah* (nonkosher). If the slaughtered animal passes all of these tests, it is declared kosher. Fish do not require any particular form of slaughter.

Glatt Kosher

Often, the inspection reveals some adhesions on the lungs of the slaughtered animal. If they can be peeled off from the lung without causing any perforations, then the animal is still kosher. The lung is tested in the same way as an auto tire, by inflating it, placing it in water, and watching for bubbles. However, some religious authorities do not permit animals whose lungs are not perfectly smooth, and many kosher consumers will not eat from animals about which such questions arose after slaughtering. Meat that is free of these problems is known as *glatt kosher*. (*Glatt* is the Yiddish word for smooth.) Because many questions arise in the process of slaughtering, meat that satisfies *glatt kosher* standards is not as widely available as regular kosher meat.

Veins and Forbidden Fats

The Torah forbids Jews to eat blood, and kosher meat goes through elaborate steps to remove all of the blood. One of the most important steps is the complete removal of the main arteries and veins where blood tends to pool, a highly skilled process called *trabering*. The Torah also forbids certain types of fat (those that were burnt sacrificially in the Temple service) from cattle, sheep, and goats, and this requires scraping off deposits of these substances from the liver, intestines, and elsewhere.

Hindquarters

The hindquarters of slaughtered animals contain not only forbidden veins and fats but also the sciatic nerve. This organ is also forbidden, because it corresponds to the "sinew that shrank," the part of the patriarch Jacob's leg that was injured when he wrestled with the angel before confronting Esau (consult Genesis 32, verses 25-33 for details). Because a high degree of skill and much expensive labor is involved in removing all of these organs, it is not economically feasible to perform it in the United States, so for all intents and purposes, the hindquarters are not used for kosher meat in this country.

Given all of the complications and restrictions involved in producing kosher meat, it is not surprising that it is generally more expensive than its nonkosher counterpart.

Koshering Meat

The next step in bringing kosher meat and poultry to the table is cleaning and salting the meat to extract the remaining forbidden blood, a process known as *koshering*, which involves soaking, salting, and rinsing the meat. Today, this is generally performed by the processor or the kosher butcher before it reaches the consumer, so that today's homemakers have it considerably easier than their mothers or grandmothers who had to kosher the meat themselves.

Liver, because it contains a large amount of blood, must be koshered in a completely different way—by broiling; because the details are quite involved, anyone who is interested in the process should consult a rabbi.

MEAT, DAIRY, AND *PAREVE*

The Torah forbids Jews from cooking or eating meat and milk foods together. This rules out such popular American combinations as a burger with a milkshake, a cheeseburger, or a pepperoni pizza. Extending the biblical restrictions, Jewish law requires that meat and dairy foods be handled separately, so that different sets of pots, dishes, cutlery, and even dishcloths and draining racks must be used to handle the two classes of foods.

Furthermore, depending on custom, Orthodox Jews wait anywhere from one hour to six hours after consuming a meat meal before they will partake of any dairy products. Jews whose families come from East European countries generally wait six hours, those from Germany wait three hours, and Dutch Jews wait only one hour.

This restriction is made easier to bear by the existence of a third class of *pareve* (neuter) foods, which contain neither meat nor dairy ingredients. Although in the old days this classification included fruits and vegetables, fish, eggs, and just about nothing else, the wonders of modern synthetic chemistry have produced many new products that greatly expand the culinary experiences available to the kosher consumer. Common examples of such *pareve* fantasy foods include imitation cheese made from tofu, synthetic bacon strips fabricated from vegetarian protein and, perhaps most important, whipped cream substitutes. Nondairy creamers and nondairy ice cream allow the Orthodox Jew to follow a meat meal with a dessert of trifle, strawberry shortcake, or ice cream with whitened coffee or capuccino.

To the kosher consumer, *pareve* foods can be considered as combining the best of both worlds. Their ever-growing diversity and availability also represents a boon to people who are not interested in the kosher aspect but are allergic to milk products. Many lactose-intolerant non-Jews have already learned that the word *pareve* on a label means that the food is totally free of dairy substances and will not trigger their allergy.

Caution: Both kosher and lactose-intolerant consumers should always remember that the term "nondairy" on a food label does not mean it is totally free of dairy ingredients, but the word *pareve*, accompanied by a reliable kosher certification, does.

OTHER PRODUCTS

Wine and Grape Juice

Wine and grape juice are only kosher when processed under strict rabbinical supervision. They must be produced and handled only by Jewish workers, and the bottles must be sealed at the plant with kosher certification on each bottle. Some well-known brands of kosher wine are Manischewitz, Kedem, Herzog, Weinstock, Carmel, Gan-Eden, and Kesser. Gourmet kosher wines that can be enjoyed by connoisseurs are produced in France, Italy, Israel, California, New York, and elsewhere.

Soft Drinks and Alcoholic Beverages

Soft drinks and beverages, including soda and juices, require rabbinical supervision because they may contain nonkosher flavorings or additives. Most major soda products, including Coca Cola, Pepsi, 7-Up and Sprite, are kosher, but many blended fruit drinks and new-age beverages are blended with nonkosher grape juice and therefore not kosher. Because the United States government enforces strict standards on the production of orange juice, a product with a label stating that it is 100% orange juice may be considered as kosher, provided it is produced in a plant that does not process other products. Thus Tropicana 100% orange juice, Minute Maid 100% orange juice, and other brands of 100% orange juice are kosher.

Liquors and blended alcoholic beverages require kosher certification, but most beer, straight whisky, scotch, and vodka are kosher. However, grape-based flavors are sometimes used here too, and some of the new beers from microbreweries use flavorings, so in general it is best to stick to kosher-approved products or, as always, to consult a rabbinical authority when in doubt.

Fresh Fruits and Vegetables

Fruits and vegetables are always kosher and *pareve*, except that Israeli-grown produce cannot be eaten by Jews until it is properly tithed, which involves removing a small portion of the produce and making a verbal declaration of the partial ownership rights of priests and Levites, which are mentioned in the Torah. When vegetables or fruits are likely to contain insects, worms, or other types of bugs, they must be washed and inspected carefully to make sure none are left. Lettuce and other leafy vegetables, such as parsley, dill, broccoli, and many others, must be inspected and washed thoroughly to remove any bugs. Frozen fruits and vegetables, provided they have no oils, sauces or other substances added in processing, are generally kosher, if they are prepared and packed in a plant that processes only kosher ingredients.

**Canned Fruits and Vegetables and
All Other Processed Foods**

Kosher supervision of both the ingredients and the processing is required for canned fruit, vegetables, and other processed foods. Many fruits and vegetables canned under major labels such as Green Giant, Dole, and Delmonte, present few kashruth problems because the products are packed in water or their own juices in a plant that does not process any nonkosher products. However, care must be taken to ensure that no oils or grape extracts are used in these facilities. In some plants that process vegetables, meats are also processed, and if canned vegetables are produced on the same machinery, they become nonkosher, even though there will be no hint of this in the list of ingredients. If there is any doubt, you can check with one of the major kash-ruth agencies, who are well informed on such issues.

Breads, Bagels, Cakes, Cookies, Pastries, and Other Baked Goods, and Cereals, Candies, and Snacks

All bakery items, cereals, candies and snacks require kosher certification to ensure that they contain no nonkosher animal fats or other animal derivatives such as gelatin. Many popular cereals from Kellogg's, Post, and General Mills are produced under kosher supervision, but some of these and other brands contain nonkosher ingredients. Grape byproducts are often used as sweeteners in health cereals. Some granolas contain gelatin or other nonkosher substances. In today's world new cereals appear and disappear with blinding speed and familiar ones are reformulated frequently; kosher consumers must, therefore, check the package for the *hechsher* (kosher certification) every time they buy.

Oils, Fats, and Margarine

Oils, fats, and margarine always require supervision. Lard and any other animal fat from a nonkosher animal are forbidden, and even pure vegetable oils or olive oil must be processed in a plant where they will not come in contact with any nonkosher oil, or with any equipment that handles nonkosher oil.

Condiments, Sauces, Preserves, Flavorings, and Spices

All condiments, sauces, preservatives, flavorings, and spices require supervision. By now, it should come as no surprise that because of the possibility that these products could come in contact during processing with nonkosher substances or equipment, a knowledgeable *mashgiach* (kosher supervisor) has to inspect the plant before it can be approved for the kosher consumer.

KOSHER FOR PASSOVER

However complex and restrictive the laws of kashruth seem to be during the year, they become much more so during the eight days of Passover, when all leavened food is forbidden. This forbidden category includes such obvious products as bread and cake as well as beer, whisky, vinegar, and other byproducts of wheat or other grains, and extends to all utensils that have come into contact with any of these substances. Essentially everything used on Passover requires special supervision, and only utensils used exclusively for Passover can be used in preparing or handling any food to be eaten during the eight-day holiday.

THE KOSHER KITCHEN

Until now, I have talked a lot about factories and food processing plants, but said nothing about the place where most kosher food is actually prepared for consumption, the home kitchen. My grandmother's kitchen in Europe looked very different from my wife's kitchen in the 1990s, but it was certainly just as kosher. Affluence has not made the world more kosher, but it has certainly made it much simpler to keep meat and milk separate and made life much easier for today's housewives.

It is not uncommon for a kosher kitchen today to have two sinks, two dishwashers and two separate counters, one for meat and one for dairy. Most people get by with one refrigerator, one stovetop, one microwave and one oven, and appropriate arrangements are made to keep meat and dairy food preparation separate. If there is only one sink that must be used for both meat and dairy purposes, dishes and cutlery cannot be put down in the sink directly, but must be washed using separate racks that keep them away from contact with the sink.

It is mandatory to have two sets of pots, cookware, dishes, and cutlery, one for meat and one for dairy. Although it is technically possible to get by with only one set of glassware (which is nonpermeable as long as it is not used for heating food), proper separation of meat and milk products requires two sets of drinking utensils if they

What Makes Food Kosher?

are made of earthenware or china, which are permeable. A third set of utensils is needed to deal with *pareve* food preparation. The approach of Passover requires a thorough cleaning of the entire kitchen and switching over to two other complete sets of pots, dishes, cutlery, and utensils devoted exclusively to Passover use.

The need for all of this equipment, in addition to the higher price of kosher meat and poultry, means that a kosher kitchen is inherently more expensive to equip and run than one that does not follow the kosher laws. It also carries with it a discipline and commitment that extends to every member of the household (even the family pet cannot be fed with pet food containing a mixture of meat and milk!). Children learn at an early age that meat is meat and milk is milk and never the twain shall meet, because it takes the cooperation of the whole family to keep a kosher kitchen.

Depending on the quantity, if milk accidentally falls into the chicken soup, not only does the soup become forbidden for consumption, but the pot becomes *treif* (nonkosher). Many metal utensils can be made kosher again by a process called *kashering*, but it may never be possible to restore your family's precious heirloom china to a kosher state if it is used incorrectly. If an earthenware or china utensil is used improperly, a qualified rabbinical authority must be consulted as to its future use.

The laws that determine exactly what makes a food mixture forbidden, when a utensil becomes nonkosher, and whether and how a utensil can be restored to a usable condition are many and complicated. Some of the factors that must be taken into account include the relative proportions of meat and milk, the temperature of the food, and how sharp the food tastes. Indeed, knowledge of details of these laws is one of the key qualifications required before an aspiring rabbi can be ordained, and answering such questions from concerned housewives is an everyday occurrence in a rabbi's life.

Kosher Eating

Kosher food alone, no matter how reliable the supervision, is not enough to make a kosher meal. After the food has been prepared in a kosher kitchen, it must be served on kosher dishes, eaten with kosher utensils and, as you have probably anticipated, the dishes served at any meal must avoid any mixture of meat and dairy foods.

As I have stressed, the kosher food laws are an expression of the Jewish religion. They are merely one part of a complete lifestyle that is dedicated to the worship of God. This means that it would be inappropriate for the observant Jew just to gobble down his food and run away; so a kosher meal consists of more than simply eating kosher food. The Torah requires that no food be consumed unless a blessing is first recited over it. The purpose of the blessing is not, as many non-Jews think, to do anything to the food, but simply to express thanks and praise to God for providing it.

The blessing before eating is not the only ritual requirement involved in eating food. If bread is to be eaten, the hands must first be washed ritually, which explains why Orthodox Jews may vanish suddenly from the table for a few minutes before commencing the meal. When the meal is finished, grace after meals is recited, which is a lengthy prayer that takes several minutes if bread was part of the meal and a shorter prayer if no bread was served.

KOSHER BLOOPERS

One of the most interesting, if not bizarre, parts of the almost quarter century I have spent in the food business is to hear the misconceptions many people have about kosher food. I can't even count the number of occasions when a manufacturer has told me, "I'd love you to taste this. Can we get the rabbi to come and bless it?" And I will never forget the time I walked into one of Washington's finest supermarkets and noticed a stack of cases of real Maryland crab soup with a kosher symbol prominently displayed on the can. When I picked up the phone and called the cannery, I was rather surprised to hear the owner tell me that he himself had decided to put the kosher symbol on the label. It seems that he also packed some spices that actually had a legitimate kosher certification symbol, and thought it would be nice to keep all the packaging uniform. That is how "kosher" crab soup appeared on the market. Oops!

There were other times I myself really goofed. For example, a customer once offered me some new potato chips to taste. Recognizing the brand name as one that was kosher, I sampled the rather greasy chips and immediately detected an unusual new taste, something foreign to my kosher palate. This is really different, I thought, and was about to dive in for more when I looked at the package again and noticed that the familiar symbol I was used to seeing on this well-known kosher brand did not appear on the label. When I inspected the bag more closely, I noticed the suddenly prominent words **FRIED IN LARD**. Oops! That was certainly a sobering experience.

Then there was the ill-fated Baltimore kosher cruise. You have certainly heard about the fatal voyage of the *Titanic*, but you have probably not heard about the disastrous evening cruise on the Chesapeake. Over 100 unsuspecting Orthodox Jews from Baltimore were enjoying a charity fundraising voyage one evening, munching on what they were sure were kosher delicacies that happened to be in the shape of imitation crab cakes. Just after leaving the harbor one unusually inquisitive soul asked a few questions and discovered that the imitation crab cakes were the real McCoy. With a sinking feeling, the passengers realized that their hometown would now be listed in the annals of Jewish history as the site of the Baltimore *treif* party. The food had been provided by the nonkosher division of a caterer who also had a kosher operation. This provided an unforgettable lesson of how careful observant Jews have to be in kosher matters.

Honest mistakes can always occur, but the person who takes kosher observance seriously doesn't feel any better afterward knowing that. To avoid mistakes, he or she must follow a few rules. If it looks even a little different, like the greasy potato chips, check the bag carefully before eating, and if still unsure, check one more time. If it sounds really crazy, like kosher real crab soup, then question it. But on a kosher cruise, how do you know that the fish cakes taste like authentic Maryland crab cakes if you have never tasted crab? Come to think of it, it may be safer to stick to more traditional Jewish cuisine like bagels and lox, gefilte fish, and kugels.

Perhaps there is only one authentic Jewish answer to my lifelong culinary quest, one that goes back to the dawn of Jewish traditions. When the Israelites wandered in the desert for 40 years after leaving Egyptian slavery, God brought down the manna (*mon* in Hebrew) from heaven. It was a bread substitute that could taste like absolutely anything the heart desired—all you had to do was wish for it. So, too, do I imagine a heavenly reward one day: a new *mon*—a universal angelic dish, flavorful, absolutely fat and cholesterol free, with zero calories. Finally, I get to experience the sensation of the Big Mac, the Whopper, the crab cake, the lobster, and even the Oreo cookie. I wonder if you can pull apart *mon* like an Oreo and scrape off the luscious creme. Who knows what golden arches lie ahead?

INVITING AN ORTHODOX GUEST TO YOUR HOME OR RESTAURANT

By far the best and easiest way to entertain your kosher guest is to take him or her to a certified kosher restaurant or other food establishment. If that is not possible, and you are hosting a party or dinner in your nonkosher home or in a nonkosher restaurant, there are things you can do to accommodate your kosher guest. Following is a set of recommendations and serving suggestions to keep in mind when serving an Orthodox person in your home:

Kosher Eating

- Always talk to your guests ahead of time to discuss foods and food preparation. Involving your guests in the advance planning will make them more comfortable at the actual event.
- Use a new or freshly laundered tablecloth.
- Use disposable paper or plastic plates, cups, and cutlery.
- Serve a sealed kosher deli or dairy (not both!) tray or platter from a certified kosher caterer or deli. Check first with your guest regarding the acceptability of the source.
- Serve uncut fresh fruit—oranges, apples, bananas, grapes, etc.
- It is acceptable to serve coffee, tea, Coke, Pepsi, 7-Up, Sprite, ginger ale, most pure 100% fruit juices (excluding any containing grape juice or derivatives), vodka, scotch, whiskey, and conventional beer.
- It is not permissible to use a nonkosher oven or stovetop. Use of a microwave *may* be permissible—but first check with your guest.
- Do not allow any kosher food to come into direct contact with the nonkosher kitchen counter or cutting boards, pots, or pans. Use only new disposable metal, paper, or plastic utensils. Do not use any previously-used kitchen utensils or knives, but only new metal or plastic cutlery. If a can opener is needed, get a new one.
- All uncooked fresh fruits and vegetables are kosher. If it is necessary to cut up fruit and vegetables, wait for your kosher guest to arrive and allow the guest to prepare or supervise all the kitchen activities. Vegetables must be thoroughly washed and inspected carefully to rid them of bugs.
- Purchase only kosher-certified foods, taking into consideration their meat or dairy status. For example, if you

are serving a kosher-certified meat platter from a local kosher deli, you may not serve a kosher dairy Entenmann's cake. It is generally a good idea to order all the food from a single kosher establishment to insure that the correct standards are met. For example, if a meat meal is being served, one must watch carefully to make sure that snacks like potato chips, nuts, and candies, besides being kosher-certified, are nondairy (*pareve*). All prepared foods, cakes, pastries, and snacks must be certified kosher. You should keep the bags, boxes, or other original containers so your guests can examine the kosher certification symbols and confirm the products' dairy or *pareve* status.

Unflavored black tea (brands like Twining's, Bigelow, Tetley, or Lipton) poses no problems, but herbal teas and flavored teas need kosher certification. Regular or decaffeinated coffee (Maxwell House, Folgers, or Sanka) are fine, but flavored coffees require kosher certification. If a meat meal is being served, a kosher nondairy (*pareve*) creamer should be used. Sweeteners (Sugar, Sweet & Low, or Equal) are generally acceptable, but check for kosher certification and, if meat is being served, for *pareve* status. One hundred percent pure orange juice, pineapple juice, and grapefruit juice are acceptable.

In some instances, glassware or glass plates may be acceptable. First check with your guest.

A kosher-certified TV dinner or airline meal, properly sealed in its container, may be heated in a nonkosher oven. Most nonkosher restaurants and caterers are able to obtain these kosher meals, but advance planning is necessary.

In circumstances in which no kosher provisions or meals are available, depending on your guests' personal standards, they may be comfortable ordering a plain salad or fruit plate. However, remember always to first consult your guests and involve them in the planning so you can accommodate their specific dietary preferences or restrictions and meet their personal religious standards of kosher certification.

Eating Out of Your Suitcase, or the Joys of Kosher Travel

Nobody ever said it was easy to be an observant Jew. And that's especially true while traveling. In fact, there are those who become less observant in direct proportion to their distance from home. That sort of behavior can bring hypocrites up short.

For example, a wise old rabbi was approached by a congregant who assured him that he kept a strictly kosher home. On the other hand, said the congregant, he did not adhere to the kosher laws in restaurants. The rabbi looked him straight in the eye and said, "So, my dear fellow, your plates will go to heaven."

Traveling abroad can present some especially difficult problems for the Orthodox Jew. My wife, Ronnie, and I have spent some interesting Sabbaths in distant and exotic places, but our visits have required some planning. In some instances, our best-laid plans have not prepared us for the complexities of keeping kosher in foreign lands.

So now, wherever we go, you can recognize us by our extra suitcase—our traveling kosher pantry.

We have found it easiest to pack an extra suitcase filled with tuna, salmon, sardines, canned meats, a box of matzoh, crackers, Entenmann cakes, paper plates, and our most precious delicacy, a nonrefrigerated smoked salami. Together with a bottle of wine and Shabbos candles with traveling candlesticks and tinfoil to place underneath them, this basic survival kit has supplied our table on many a trip.

I remember a beautiful sunset Sabbath dinner overlooking Hong Kong Bay. We decorated our room table with flowers, sang Sabbath songs, and watched the boats floating by in the bay below. And I will never forget the Friday night in Souchow, China, when we brought the Sabbath candles to our table in the hotel dining room and lit them there. As the candles began to burn, we suddenly found ourselves surrounded by six Chinese waiters who broke into a chorus of "Happy Birthday."

On Sabbath we refrain from using elevators. I remember shortly after we were married we were assigned a hotel room on the eighth floor. Late Friday night we began our journey up eight steep flights. Exhausted, we finally reached our room door and I requested the key from my wife. She looked at me and I looked at her and 16 flights later I collapsed on the bed with the hotel's spare key in my hand. Now we always request a low floor for Shabbos.

It is always a good idea to arrive at your hotel early on Friday so you can make the necessary Sabbath arrangements. Check out the hotel staircases, and make sure you can use them. One Shabbos in Tokyo, we realized that the self-locking staircase doors only opened out onto the hotel floors, making it possible for us to go from our floor to the staircase but impossible to get back inside again on another floor. Trying to explain our dilemma to the hotel manager was an exercise in futility. The manager assured me that the elevators were quite safe. We finally took matters into our own hands and placed metal ashtrays between each door and its frame for seven flights. These door stoppers prevented the doors from locking and enabled us to reach our seventh floor room. We are still trying to figure out who yanked out the fourth floor ash tray. It meant that we had to locate a non-Jew to take the elevator to the fourth floor and open the door.

Another hurdle is posed by the electronic doors that frequently serve as hotels' main entrances. When we encounter one on Shabbos we have to wait until another guest activates the door. Then we politely dash inside after the surprised door-opener.

As if the door problem is not bad enough, some hotels have electronic room pass cards that operate your room door. Most establishments have dual key systems and a standard key can be obtained from the front desk, but it takes careful negotiations. Many a hotel clerk has gazed strangely at my wife and me as we tried to explain our situation.

Imagine the perplexed bellhop who delivers a package to your room on Shabbos. Not only do you have the chutzpah not to tip the poor soul, but you give him a hard time when he asks for a signature. Bewildered, he suggests we call the front desk. After all, he's only doing his job. All he wants is proof of delivery. After we explain to him that the phone is off limits, he suggests we both go downstairs to straighten out the problem. What could be going through his mind as he heads for the elevator and I explain that I'm taking the stairs?

Praying is generally not a big problem. One can pray privately in a hotel room. For short prayers, a telephone booth is private enough, as long as there are other empty booths available for paying customers who actually want to use the phone. Moving one's lips in a phone booth with a phone set to your head looks quite natural. Who is to know that the Almighty is on the other end of the line?

At the Peking guest house in China a servant would enter my room every morning with a fresh pot of tea, just as I was reciting my morning prayers, wearing my tefillin (black leather boxes containing scriptural verses that Orthodox Jews strap to their heads and arms during morning prayers). Staring at the black straps on my arms, he thought I was taking my blood pressure.

There have been occasions when time restrictions made praying an urgent matter. Once on Japan Air Lines I asked a steward for permission to use one of the plane's kitchens to perform my morning prayers. Drawing the curtain closed, I wrapped myself in my tallis (prayer shawl) and tefillin and began to pray. Pulling back the curtain, a terrified stewardess drew back in alarm, suspecting that I was a terrorist who had wired myself to commandeer the plane. She screamed, and in a flash all the passengers reached a state of near-panic. She calmed down after other crew members assured her I was merely serving my Creator, and in a short while the frantic passengers settled down too. Neither the stewardess nor I will ever forget the incident.

At Aswan Airport in Egypt I explained to the commanding officer of airport security that the little black boxes were my tefillin. He examined the boxes carefully. An Egyptian I was traveling with warned me that it would be better to pray in the middle of the airport, fully visible to all, rather than to go off to a corner or a small room where security might suspect terrorist activity. Veiled in religious garb, and surrounded by the airport's bustling population, and under the careful watch of the Egyptian armed forces, I said my morning prayers.

Chinese officials also gave me a hard time with tefillin, but after strenuous negotiations they allowed my prayer utensils to enter the People's Republic of China. My can of Lysol was not so lucky and was confiscated.

At London's prestigious Claridge's, where kings, queens, presidents, prime ministers, and heads of state stay when in town, we were greeted by a staff in high-hats and long-tail coats. Claridge's is known for its exquisite cuisine and impeccable service, and is equipped with a kitchen on each floor to insure superb 24-hour room service. We must have been a sight to behold on Friday afternoon when we entered London's finest address shlepping our bulging bags of kosher Shabbos provisions from Bloom's Kosher Restaurant in London. It was quite evident that the elevator concierge had never before been exposed to the aroma of Shabbos chicken, kugel, and our succulent kosher dill pickles. I'm sure that the Claridge's elevators still bear a garlic aroma to this day.

In Hong Kong our group of 60 gourmets was personally greeted by the president of the Hong Kong Country Club. This Chinese gentleman was an extremely wealthy industrialist whose family ran one of the largest textile empires in the Far East.

Traveling with my own provisions, I was quite content to open my can of sardines, order a drink and fresh fruit, and admire the beauty and ambiance of this beautiful setting. But the host had anticipated my situation. Taking note of my yarmulke, he greeted me with a warm smile and led me into his kitchen. There, the master chef was awaiting me, and proudly displayed his preparations. On tinfoil three layers thick lay a fresh brook trout.

My host pointed out that the fish had both fins and scales. Using a brand new knife, the chef began to fillet the fish. He seasoned it with pepper, paprika, and lemon, and basted it with butter. He triple-wrapped the fresh fish and vegetables in tinfoil with the same seasoning. A fresh fruit cup was also prepared and topped with fresh raspberries.

The preparation met every qualification of kosher observance. We were served on paper plates with plastic cutlery. The food came to the table hot and still triple-wrapped in foil, and I must say it was a kosher culinary delight.

Amazed, I asked my Chinese host where he had learned his kosher food preparations. As it turned out, the president of the Hong Kong Country Club, had attended the University of Pennsylvania's Wharton School of Business. His roommate for four years was a *shomer shabbos*, a Sabbath observer. The two students kept a kosher kitchen in the room for all four years, and my host was not only very familiar with kashruth but also knew about the Sabbath and all of the Jewish holidays and other customs.

Ironically, the next evening at the Tokyo Jewish Community Center, we realized that the food we were served was only "kosher style" and not really kosher.

I do not recommend that observant Jews eat in non-kosher restaurants. Extreme care must be taken to ensure that all food preparations are in complete conformity with halacha (Jewish law). Unless there is a *mashgiach* (kosher supervisor) on the premises, and there are complete kosher facilities, one should avoid eating out.

Throughout my business career, I have had kitchen privileges in some of the best restaurants and hotels and am often able to personally cater my own kosher cuisine. At one 700-guest dinner at the Sheraton Washington, I entertained a party of ten guests. At my table four people received kosher airline dinners, while the other six were served the nonkosher dinner. The Sheraton provided our entire table with brand new china and new cutlery so that the kosher airline dinner could be served on fine china. With the help of the food and beverage manager, our dinner was equal, in both quality and presentation, with the general dinner served that evening.

But even with careful planning, things don't always go your way. For an elaborate banquet in one of Atlanta's best hotels, I requested a kosher airline dinner two weeks in advance. The waiter brought me a fish dinner cooked by the hotel—their idea of a kosher dinner. After I explained that the fish dinner was not kosher because it was not prepared in a true kosher environment, the hotel staff brought me a lettuce plate and some fresh fruit. The dinner cost me $75, rather expensive for lettuce and fresh fruit. Since then, I have learned to be very specific about my kosher needs.

In most European countries, kosher food and synagogues are readily available, and life for the Orthodox Jew is just like home. Advance planning is suggested, and publications such as the *Jewish Travel Guide* (718-972-9010), *Kashrus Magazine* (718-336-8544) and *The Jewish Traveler* (410-484-1957) are excellent tools for finding kosher restaurants and synagogues anywhere in the world.

Bon Voyage! Have a marvelous trip.

Summing Up

In the preceding pages, I have tried to describe my Orthodox Jewish world and my tradition. Do you now understand everything about Orthodox Judaism? Of course not! But you understand a little more than you did before. Now you may not regard me as so strange if you ever run across me mumbling to myself after lunch, or notice my yarmulke when I put it on before eating or drinking or if I wear it all the time at the office.

You also appreciate that when I leave work early, or take off days at unusual times of the year, I'm not trying to escape from the real world of work, but striving to maintain a connection with a different but equally real world of traditional laws and beliefs. That world is built on a set of laws and customs that have been handed down from parents to children for thousands of years. One of the main goals of my life is to bring up my children so they, too, are at home in it. I take my work very seriously, but I know that if I want my children to follow in the age-old traditions of my family, I have to show them by actions as well as words that keeping those traditions is a very serious lifelong commitment, seven days a week.

Remember, next time you see me checking out a line of phone booths to make sure I won't be inconveniencing any waiting people, then going into one to stand and sway, I may be praying instead of talking into the phone. I'm not using AT&T, Sprint, or MCI, but I am making a long-distance connection. There's no charge for the call and, most importantly, there's never an answering device at the other end of the line; one thing about the Lord—He's always home.

Glossary of Hebrew and Yiddish Terms

Aravos: Stems of willow trees. Two stems are included as one of the Four Species taken during religious services on Sukkos.

Aron Kodesh: Holy Ark. Cabinet where Torah scrolls are kept.

Avreich(im): Young married graduate yeshiva student(s).

Badeken: Ceremonial covering of the bride's head by a veil, performed by the groom at Orthodox weddings.

Bar Mitzvah: Arrival of a Jewish male at the status of a legally responsible adult. Occurs automatically on the thirteenth birthday. Usually marked by calling to the Torah reading in synagogue; often followed by a festive meal.

Bas Mitzvah: Arrival of a Jewish female at the status of a legally responsible adult. Occurs automatically on the twelfth birthday. Often celebrated by a festive meal.

Bimah: Platform or table in the center of an Orthodox synagogue used for public reading of the Torah during services.

Bnai Brak: Orthodox community in Israel situated close to Tel Aviv.

Bochur: Unmarried yeshivah student. (Plural form: Bochurim.)

Bris: See Bris Milah.

Bris Milah: Circumcision. Normally performed on eighth day after birth, but may be delayed for health reasons.

Chabad: Acronym made up of initials of Hebrew words *Chochmah*, *Binah*, and *Daas*, which refer to three types of wisdom. Alternative name for the Chassidic movement usually known as *Lubavitch*.

Chanukah: Eight-day festival, celebrated by candle-lighting, which commemorates miraculous victory of the Maccabees.

Chasan: Hebrew word for bridegroom.

Chassid: Adherent of religious movement founded in eighteenth century. Chassidim follow charismatic leaders called *rebbes*. Many Chassidim dress in distinctive clothing.

Chassidim: Plural form of Chassid.

Chesed: Good deeds.

Chol Hamoed: Intermediate days of the Passover and Sukkos festivals, when necessary work is permitted.

Cholent: Stew left cooking overnight to provide hot food on the Sabbath.

Cholov Yisroel: Milk produced under direct observation of an Orthodox Jew.

Chometz: Any form of leavened food. All chometz is forbidden on Passover.

Chuppah: Canopy under which bride and groom stand during Jewish wedding ceremony.

Chutzpah: Unmitigated gall. The classic example is the apocryphal juvenile delinquent who killed his parents and pleaded for mercy because he was an orphan.

Daven: To pray (Yiddish).

Derech Eretz: Hebrew term that can refer to manners, culture, refined behavior, or earning a living.

Dreidel: Four-sided spinning top played with on Chanukah.

Eretz Yisroel: The Land of Israel

Eruv: Symbolic enclosure to permit carrying within it on the Sabbath.

Esrog: Citron, a lemon-like fruit that is one of the Four Species taken during religious services on Sukkos.

Frum: Orthodox (Yiddish).

Gemilus Chasodim: Helping other people personally in ways other than donating money.

Glatt Kosher: Meat from an animal whose lungs have been inspected and found free from adhesions.

Hadassim: Willow twigs. Three such twigs make up one of the Four Species taken during religious services on Sukkos.

Halacha: The corpus of Jewish law as decided by the Talmud and later codes and rabbinical authorities.

Haman: Persian vizier who plotted to exterminate all the Jews in the Persian Empire. His miraculous downfall is celebrated on Purim.

Havdalah: Home ritual held to mark the end of the Sabbath, involving recital of blessings over wine, fragrant spices, and a braided candle. It is also recited in the synagogue at the end of the evening service after the Sabbath.

Hechsher: Certificate of acceptability of kosher food provided by a rabbi.

Hesped: Eulogy.

Horeb: Alternative name for Mount Sinai; name of book by Rabbi Samson Raphael Hirsch.

Hoshana Rabbah: Seventh day of Sukkos.

Kaddish: Aramaic prayer praising God that is recited at the end of every section of communal prayer services. It is also recited by mourners at the gravesite and at the end of each of the daily prayer services. It is not recited in the absence of a minyan.

Kallah: Bride.

Kashering: Making utensils acceptable for use with kosher food.

Kashrus (Kashruth): Abstract noun corresponding to the adjective "Kosher."

Kiddush: Sanctification prayer recited before the evening and morning meals on the Sabbath and Festivals; also used for a sometimes lavish repast served following that prayer after the Shabbos morning prayers, to be followed some time later by the main meal.

Kinnos (Kinnot): Dirges recited on Tishah B'Av to commemorate the destruction of the Holy Temple and other historical tragedies of the Jewish people.

Kohen (pl. Kohanim): Member of a priestly family descended from Moses's brother Aaron.

Koshering: Soaking, salting, and rinsing kosher-slaughtered meat or poultry to make it kosher to eat.

Kugel: Pudding-like dish made from potatoes, rice, noodles, etc. Usually eaten on the Sabbath.

Latkes: Fried potato pancakes eaten on Chanukah.

Levites: Members of a family descended from the tribe of Levi.

Lubavitch: See Chabad.

Lulav: Palm branch. One of the Four Species taken during religious services on Sukkos.

Maccabees: Family that led the uprising against the Syrian-Greeks that culminated in the victory celebrated by Chanukah.

Maror: Bitter herbs eaten at the Passover seder to symbolize the bitterness of slavery in Egypt.

Matzoh: Flat (unleavened) bread eaten at the Passover seder and during the entire Passover holiday to recall the Exodus from Egypt.

Mazal Tov: Exclamation, meaning "Good Luck!" made at all happy occasions.

Mechitzah: Partition to separate men and women in synagogue and at some social functions.

Mikvah: Ritual bath house used regularly by married women; immersion in a mikvah is also a required part of the conversion ceremony.

Mikvaos: Ritual bath houses used by married women in following the laws of family purity.

Minhag: A custom that has been accepted among a group of Jews. If a *minhag* becomes accepted widely enough, it may achieve the status of a religious law.

Minyan: Quorum of ten men needed to recite communal prayers.

Mitzvah: One of the 613 commandments mentioned in the Torah or listed by the rabbis of the Talmud.

Mohel: Man who performs circumcisions.

Mordechai: Leader of the Jewish people at the time of the Purim miracle. Uncle and mentor of Queen Esther.

Mon: Manna, the miraculous food from heaven that sustained the Children of Israel for 40 years in the wilderness, following the Exodus. Jewish tradition teaches that its taste mirrored that of any food desired by the person eating it.

Pareve: Foodstuff with neither meat nor dairy ingredients.

Payos: "Corners" of the head which may not be shaved with a razor. Long earlocks worn by Chassidim and some other Orthodox Jews.

Pesach: Passover.

Rebbe: (1) Leader of a Chassidic group. (2) Term of respect used by students of all ages to refer to their teacher of Jewish religious subjects.

Rosh Hashana: Solemn two-day holiday celebrating the Jewish New Year.

Rosh Yeshiva: Distinguished Talmudic scholar who heads a higher yeshivah.

Sefer Torah: Scroll used for public reading of the Torah. It must be handwritten in the traditional Hebrew script on parchment by a pious and skilled scribe using a quill pen.

Shabbos (Shabbat): The Sabbath.

Shavuos (Shavuoth): The Feast of Weeks, or Pentecost. One of the three major festivals, it begins seven weeks after the second day of Passover. In Israel, it is a one-day festival, but lasts two days outside Israel.

Shechitah: The method of slaughtering animals required by Jewish law to make them kosher.

Sheitel: Wig worn by Orthodox women to avoid transgressing the prohibition on uncovered hair.

Shemini Atzeres: The eighth day of the Sukkos holiday. Technically, it is a separate holiday. (The Eighth Day of Solemn Assembly.)

Shivah: Seven days of mourning observed for close relatives (Father, mother, husband, wife, brother, sister, or child).

Shochet: Ritual slaughterer; a pious Jew who is proficient in the laws of shechitah.

Shomer Shabbos: A Sabbath observer.

Shul: Synagogue (Yiddish).

Shulchan Aruch: The authoritative code of Jewish Law followed by Orthodox Jews, written by Rabbi Joseph Karo in the fifteenth century.

Simcha: A happy occasion, like a wedding, Bar Mitzvah, or Bris.

Simchas Torah: The joyful festival on which the annual cycle of reading the Torah is completed. It falls on the day after Shemini Atzeres (technically, the second day of that festival) outside Israel, and on Shemini Atzeres in Israel.

Sukkah: Temporary hut with a roof made of branches or bamboo in which Orthodox Jews eat (and some sleep) during Sukkos.

Sukkos: One of the three major festivals. Lasts seven days, and is followed immediately by Shemini Atzeres and Simchas Torah.

Tabernacle: Structure that served as the center of religious observances while the Children of Israel were wandering in the wilderness and was the prototype for the Holy Temple in Jerusalem. Activities performed in constructing the Tabernacle define the 39 categories of work prohibited on the Sabbath.

Taiglech: Very hard sweet confection eaten on Rosh Hashana.

Tallis: Prayer shawl with *tzitzis* worn by men (and sometimes boys) during morning prayers.

Glossary of Hebrew and Yiddish Terms

Talmud: Key document of the Oral Law, which explains and amplifies the laws of the Torah.

Tefillin: Phylacteries: Two black leather boxes containing scriptural passages worn strapped to the head and left arm by men during weekday morning prayers.

Tisha B'Av: Full 25-hour day of fasting to mourn the destruction of the two Temples in Jerusalem and other historic tragedies.

Trabering: Porging: Removing from a kosher-slaughtered animal of arteries, veins, fats, and sinews that may not be eaten.

Treif: Nonkosher (colloquial).

Treifah: An animal (or human) with a fatal condition.

Tzedakah: Charitable giving.

Tzimmes: Sweet dish made from cooked carrots.

Tzitzis: Ritual fringes on edges of four-cornered garment worn by Orthodox Jews to fulfill biblical commandment.

Yarmulke: Skull cap worn by Orthodox Jews to cover their head when they are not (and also sometimes when they are) wearing a hat.

Yeshivah: (1) Rabbinical seminary.
(2) Jewish Orthodox all-day elementary or high school.

Yiddish: Everyday language used by Eastern European Jews, based on German but with a large content of Hebrew words. It is written using the Hebrew alphabet.

Yom Kippur: Day of Atonement. The holiest day of the Jewish year, when Jews fast for 25 hours, refrain from work, and spend the day in synagogue repenting their sins and praying for forgiveness.

Yom Tov: A Jewish holiday when work is forbidden.

Yungeleit: Young, married men, especially those still studying Talmud full-time.

Index

Airlines, 84-85
Alcoholic beverages, kosher food requirements, 67
Animal species, kosher food requirements, 60
Arteries, kosher food requirements, 63

Bakery items, kosher food requirements, 68
Bar Mitzvah and Bat Mitzvah, described, 38-39
Beverages, kosher food requirements, 66-67

Blessing. See Kiddush (blessing)
Blood, kosher food requirements, 63, 64
Breads, kosher food requirements, 68
Bris (circumcision), described, 38
Business activity
 holiday restrictions, 35-36
 Passover celebration, 33
 Sabbath (Shabbos), 25-26
 Sukkos celebration, 31

Cakes, kosher food
    requirements, 68
Candies, kosher food
    requirements, 68
Candles, Sabbath
    (*Shabbos*)
    celebration, 20-21
Canned fruits and
    vegetables, kosher
    food requirements,
    67-68
Celebrations, 37-46
    Bar Mitzvah and Bat
        Mitzvah, 38-39
    bris (circumcision), 38
    clothing and behavior,
        37
    courtship, 39-42
    funerals, 45-46
    weddings, 43-45
Chanukah, described, 34
Charity and good deeds
    (*tzedakah* and
    chesed), Orthodox
    Judaism, 9-11
Chassidic Jews
    customs, 9
    described, 13-14
    Shidduch process, 42
Cheese
    kosher food
        requirements, 61
    meats and, prohibition,
        64-66

Chesed. See Charity and
    good deeds
    (*tzedakah* and
    chesed)
Child, Julia, 51
Chuppah, wedding
    ceremony, 43-45
Circumcision (*bris*),
    described, 38
Citron (*esrog*), Sukkos
    celebration, 31
Cleaning, kosher food
    requirements, 64
Clothing
    celebrations, 37
    Chassidic Jews, 9, 14
    customs, 9
    Orthodox Jews, 15
    shatnez, 8
Commandments, laws
    and customs
    (*mitzvos* and
    minhagim), 7-9
Condiments, kosher food
    requirements, 69
Conservative Judaism, 2,
    13
Conversion, to Judaism, 1
Cookies, kosher food
    requirements, 68
Courtship, described,
    39-42
Creation, Sabbath
    (*Shabbos*) and, 17

Index

Dairy foods, meats and, prohibition, 64–66
Death, funerals, 45–46
D'Ermo, Dominique, 50
Dietary laws. *See* Kosher laws
Divorce, Orthodox Jews, 42

Earlocks (*payos*), Chassidic Jews, 14
Education. *See* Religious education; Torah study
Eggs, kosher food requirements, 61
Emergency situations, Sabbath (*Shabbos*), 26–27
Eruv, Sabbath (*Shabbos*), 23–25
Exodus, Passover celebration, 32–33

Family life, Sabbath (*Shabbos*) celebration, 21–22
Fats, kosher food requirements, 63, 69
Fish, kosher food requirements, 60
Flavorings, kosher food requirements, 69
Four species, Sukkos celebration, 31

Fowler, Wick, 51
Fruits and vegetables, kosher food requirements, 67–68
Funerals, described, 45–46

Glatt kosher, defined, 62–63
God-human relationship, Orthodox Judaism, 2–3
Gourmet foods, kosher laws and, 49–51, 53–54
Grape juice, kosher food requirements, 66
Guests, kosher laws, 76–79

Health concerns, kosher laws and, 54–55
Hindquarters, kosher food requirements, 63–64
Hirsch, Samson Raphael, 3
Holidays, 29–36
   business activity restrictions during, 35–36
   Chanukah, 34
   kosher laws, 48–49
   Passover, 32–33
   Purim, 34
   Rosh Hashana, 29–30
   Shavuos, 33–34
   Sukkos, 30–32

Holidays (continued)
  Tisha B'Av, 35
  Yom Kippur, 30
Holy Ark (*Aron Kodesh*),
  synagogue service, 6
Hotels, Sabbath
  (*Shabbos*), 82–83

Israel (modern state),
  Orthodox Judaism
  and, 11

Jardine, Dan, 50
Jewish education. *See*
  Religious education
Judaism
  groupings within, 2
  Torah and, 1–2

Kashering, 71
Kiddush (blessing)
  foods, 73–74
  Sabbath (*Shabbos*)
    celebration, 21
Kitchen requirements,
  kosher laws, 70–72
Kosher laws, 47–87
  error and, 74–76
  food products, 51–54
  food requirements,
    57–72
    animal species, 60
    bakery items, 68
    beverages, 66–67
    cheese, 61
    condiments, sauces,
      preserves,
      flavorings and
      spices, 69
    fruits and vegetables,
      67–68
    generally, 57–60
    meat and dairy
      prohibition,
      64–66
    meats, 61–64
    milk and eggs, 61
    oils, fats, and
      margarine, 69
    Passover, 69–70
  gourmet foods and,
    49–51
  guests, 76–79
  health concerns and,
    54–55
  kitchen requirements,
    70–72
  Orthodox Judaism, 2, 9
  overview of, 47–48
  Passover celebration,
    32
  rationale for, 55–56
  serving requirements,
    73–74
  Shavuos celebration, 34
  symbols, 52, 58–59
  tradition and, 48–51
  travel and, 81–87

Index

Labeling, kosher laws, 74–76
Language, Chassidic Jews, 14
Lard, kosher food requirements, 69, 75
Laws and customs (*mitzvos* and *minhagim*), Orthodox Judaism, 7–9
Liver, kosher food requirements, 64
Lubavitch group, Chassidic Jews, 14

Male-female relationships
  celebrations, 37
  Chassidic Jews, 14
  courtship, 39–42
  Orthodox Judaism, 6, 15
  religious education, 7
  Sabbath (*Shabbos*) celebration, 20–21
Margarine, kosher food requirements, 69
Matzoh, Passover celebration, 32, 48
Meats
  dairy foods and, prohibition, 64–66
  kosher food requirements, 60, 61–64

Messianism, Orthodox Judaism, 2
Milk
  kosher food requirements, 61
  meats and, prohibition, 64–66
Minhagim. See Laws and customs (*mitzvos* and *minhagim*)
Mitzvos. See Laws and customs (*mitzvos* and *minhagim*)
Modesty, clothing, 37
Mourning (*shivah*), funerals, 45–46
Myrtle twigs (*hadassim*), Sukkos celebration, 31

Oils, kosher food requirements, 69
Olive oil, kosher food requirements, 69
Orange juice, kosher food requirements, 66
Orthodox Judaism
  behavior and, xv–xvii
  celebrations of, 37–46. *See also* Celebrations
  charity and good deeds (*tzedakah* and *chesed*), 9–11

Orthodox Judaism
(*continued*)
  Chassidic Jews, 13–14
  defined, 1–3, 15–16
  holidays, 29–36. *See also* Holidays
  Israel (modern state) and, 11
  Kosher laws, 47–87. *See also* Kosher laws
  laws and customs (*mitzvos* and *minhagim*), 7–9
  non-Chassidic Jews, 15–16
  prayer, 5
  Sabbath (*Shabbos*), 17–27
  synagogue, 6
  Torah study and education, 6–7

Palm stalk (*lulav*), Sukkos celebration, 31
Pareve foods, kosher laws, meat and dairy prohibition, 65–66
Passover
  described, 32–33
  kosher laws, 48, 69–70
Pastries, kosher food requirements, 68

Payos. See Earlocks (*payos*)
Phylacteries (*tefillin*), 39, 84–85
Physicians, Sabbath (*Shabbos*), 26
Poultry, kosher food requirements, 60
Prayer
  Orthodox Judaism, 5
  travel and, 84
Preserves, kosher food requirements, 69
Processed foods, kosher food requirements, 67–68
Prudhomme, Paul, 50, 51
Purim, described, 34

Reform Judaism, 2, 13
Religious education, Orthodox Judaism, 6–7, 15
Restaurants
  kosher laws, 76–79
  travel and, 85–87
Rosh Hashana
  described, 29–30
  kosher laws, 48

Sabbath (*Shabbos*), 17–27
  business activity, 25–26
  defined, 17–18

Index

emergency situations, 26–27
eruv, 23–25
kosher laws, 48–49
observance of, 18–20
Orthodox Judaism, 2
prohibitions, 22–23
travel and, 82–83, 85
typical celebration of, 20–22
Salting, kosher food requirements, 64
Sauces, kosher food requirements, 69
Sciatic nerve, kosher food requirements, 63
Secular Judaism, 2
Seder, Passover celebration, 32–33
Shatnez, 8
Shavuos
  described, 33–34
  kosher laws, 48
Shidduch process, courtship, 40–42
Shiluach Haken, 8–9
Shivah (mourning), funerals, 45–46
Slaughter (*shechitah*), kosher food requirements, 61–63
Soft drinks, kosher food requirements, 66
Spices, kosher food requirements, 69
Sukkos, described, 30–32
Symbols, kosher foods, 52, 58–59
Synagogue
  Orthodox Judaism, 6, 37
  Sabbath (*Shabbos*) celebration, 21
  Sukkos celebration, 31–32

Tefillin (phylacteries), 39, 84–85
Tisha B'Av, described, 35
Tithing, charity and good deeds (*tzedakah* and *chesed*), 10
Torah
  food blessing, 73
  Judaism and, 1–2
  laws and customs (*mitzvos* and *minhagim*), 7–9
  Orthodox Judaism and, 13
  Shavuos celebration, 33–34
  synagogue service, 6
Torah study, Orthodox Judaism, 6–7
Trabering, kosher food requirements, 63

Travel, kosher laws and, 81–87
Treif, 71
Twining, Sam, 51
Tzedakah. *See* Charity and good deeds (*tzedakah* and *chesed*)

Vegetable oil, kosher food requirements, 69
Vegetables. *See* Fruits and vegetables
Veins, kosher food requirements, 63

Weddings, described, 43–45
Wigs, Orthodox Jews, 15
Willow branches (*aravos*), Sukkos celebration, 31
Wine, kosher food requirements, 66
Work. *See* Business activity

Yarmulke
   celebrations, 37
   meaning of, xv–xvi
Yiddish, Chassidic Jews, 14
Yom Kippur, described, 30

About the Author

Eli W. Schlossberg is a Baltimore business executive and community leader.

Mr. Schlossberg attended Orthodox Jewish day schools for twelve years and spent four post-high school years studying in yeshivoth (rabbinical seminaries) in the United States and Israel. He received his formal business education from Loyola College of Baltimore, Maryland. While serving as CEO of a family gourmet food distribution business for fifteen years, he traveled extensively in Europe, Asia, and the Middle East.

Since selling the family company in 1987, Mr. Schlossberg has been a consultant to the gourmet food industry and has served as CEO of another gourmet distribution company. Currently, he is Regional Sales Director for the Mid-Atlantic States for Gourmet Award Foods of Albany, New York. In addition to his business endeavors, Mr. Schlossberg plays an active role in Jewish communal affairs and many charitable projects including Ahavas Yisrael, a Baltimore kosher food bank. He resides in Baltimore with his wife, Ronnie.

This book was edited by Jeffrey Marsh, who has worked as a physicist, policy analyst, management consultant, and corporate speechwriter. He is President of Marsh Communications, Inc., a Baltimore consulting firm. Dr. Marsh served as Chairman of the Baltimore Bureau of Kosher Meat and Food Control.

Mr. Schlossberg resides in Baltimore with his wife, Ronnie, and his two children, Mark and Michelle.

This book was edited by Jeffrey Marsh, who has worked as a physicist, policy analyst, management consultant, and corporate speechwriter. He is president of Marsh Communications, Inc., a Baltimore consulting firm. Dr. Marsh served as chairman of the Baltimore Bureau of Kosher Meat and Food Control.

www.ingramcontent.com/pod-product-compliance
Lightning Source LLC
Chambersburg PA
CBHW030117010526
44116CB00005B/282